Rue St Jacques

Rue

Bd

d Pasteur

Bd Ca

CW00421580

Gare
e Eu

Rue des Arts

Rue L Trulin

Carnot

Rue de Paris

Avenue

EURALILLE

T

Gare
Lille Flandres

Av. Willy Brandt

Rue Faidherbe

✕ Église
St Maurice

Rue des Tanneurs

au Molinel

Rue E Delesalle

Rue de Paris

Rue Gustave Delory

Av C St Venant

Rue de Tournai

Rue

Boulevard L

Av du Pres J F Kennedy

Mairie
de Lille

Rue C Debierre

art

Rue
Malpart

Rue
Sauv

G Lefe

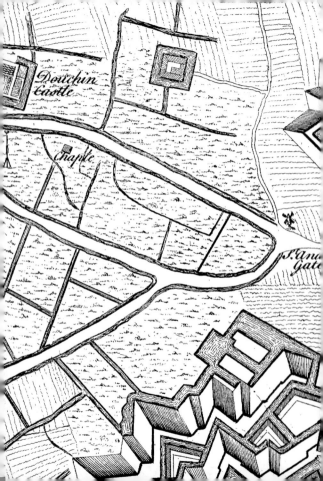

Douchin Castle

Chaple

S. And. Gate

LILLE
for Pleasure

Derek Blyth

PALLAS ATHENE

CONTENTS

Pleasures of Lille

I. Pleasures of Lille. On my first visit to Lille in early 1993, I was utterly seduced by this northern French town. I had gone, as most people probably do, expecting to find a dull provincial place, perhaps with a small art gallery, an interesting church or two, but not much else of interest. I had not at all anticipated the beautiful cobbled streets of Vieux Lille, or the lovely Dutch kitchen in the Hospice Comtesse, or the astonishing renaissance courtyard of the Vieille Bourse, or the sophisticated automated metro, or the gorgeous shop interiors on the Rue Esquermoise.

I was unprepared, too, for the uncommon vitality of this town. After wandering around the streets of Vieux Lille for several hours, I finally arrived on the main square at about six on a wet Friday evening, expecting it to be deserted, like most northern French towns. Yet it was astonishingly lively, with people coming out of the huge Furet du Nord bookshop, strolling off to see a film in the Rue de Béthune, or squeezing into the cafés facing the old stock exchange. It felt, in a way, more like somewhere in Italy, rather than a provincial French town on a rainy winter evening.

I did not realise it at the time, but Lille had just gone through a renaissance. Up until the early 1980's, it had been a depressed northern industrial town with little hope of recovery. The local textile industry had collapsed, the seventeenth-century façades of the old town were crumbling in the rain, and the population had declined dramatically from 212,000 in 1900 to 172,000 in 1975.

Then a little miracle happened. On 20 January 1986, Mrs Thatcher, prime minister of Great Britain, arrived in Lille, handbag firmly clutched. She was taken to the town hall, where she sat down next to François Mitterand, president of France, and announced that the two countries had agreed to build the Channel Tunnel. After two centuries of aborted plans, France and England were to be joined by a rail tunnel.

That might have been the end of it, Lille's five minutes of fame, but the mayor of Lille, Pierre Mauroy, had bigger plans. He immediately launched a campaign to persuade the government to build a

new high-speed train station in Lille. The railway authorities had set their minds on a site in the beet fields outside Amiens, but Mauroy (above, in front of his creation) was determined to have the station in Lille, on the edge of the historic city, just beyond the seventeenth-century fortifications. It took a long battle, but Mauroy finally got his way. He then pressed ahead with the construction of Euralille, an ambitious business and shopping complex strategically sited next to the new station.

And there was more to Lille's revival than high-speed travel and modern architecture. Since the late

1970's, the city had been renovating the historic quarters of Vieux Lille, turning mouldering slum houses and dank courtyards into elegant boutiques and restaurants. By the time the high-speed trains started to run between London and Paris in 1994, the restoration of Vieux Lille was almost completed. The timing was just perfect; tourists stepping off the Eurostar to take a look at Lille discovered a city they had never imagined.

The novelty has now perhaps worn off. Some elements of the new architecture have proved a mistake, such as the bleak platforms at Lille-Europe station and the unimaginative interior of the Euralille shopping centre. Yet Lille has continued to improve over the past decade, investing heavily in the restoration of the Vieille Bourse, creating a new urban promenade along the Quai de Wault, and turning the Palais des Beaux-Arts into one of the most exhilarating art galleries in Europe.

Despite all the changes, Lille continues to offer visitors the peculiar pleasures of a provincial French town. We will find cafés with round marble tables, convivial street markets that sell cheeses from the Nord region, handsome boulevards shaded by plane trees and elegant designer shops. Yet there is something else to Lille, something that reminds visitors of

Brussels and Antwerp. It might not strike us on arrival, as we step off the Eurostar into a chilly gust of wind, but we just have to walk ten minutes to the main square to find Flemish architecture, cafés serving Duvel and Hoegaarden beers, and restaurants with Belgian dishes such as moules-frites, waterzooi and carbonnade à la Flamande on the menu. The Flemish influence is perhaps only to be expected, as the frontier lies just a few kilometres away, a short walk from the last stop on the métro line. However, the links with Flanders go much deeper, since Lille was part of Flanders for many centuries. It was ruled first by the Counts of Flanders and then the Dukes of Burgundy, becoming famous throughout Europe for its spectacular religious processions and banquets that went on for days. It was not until the late seventeenth century that the citizens of Lille became French, and had to learn to obey regulations issued in Paris. Yet long after the city had adopted French laws and customs, Lille continued to have close ties to Belgium; the first railway line was built from Lille to Ghent and Antwerp, four years before the line to Paris was completed.

Lille, then, is something of a mongrel town. It has seventeenth-century Flemish quarters, harmonious eighteenth-century French areas, and a striking

13

modern business district. All of this makes it far live-lier than most provincial French towns, a place where you can eat moules and frites in a Art Deco brasserie, buy tulips in a Flemish renaissance courtyard, watch a Spanish film with French subtitles, sit in a patch of late-afternoon sunshine drinking a dark Flanders ale, and sleep in a hotel that was once a mediaeval hospice.

II. Arriving in Lille. People tend to arrive by Eurostar or Thalys train at Lille Europe station (though some may come from Paris by TGV and arrive at the old Lille-Flandres station). The new station is, as Mauroy insisted that it had to be, just a short walk from the centre of Lille, yet it is a some-what confusing place. We can, of course, simply take a taxi to our hotel, and our problems will be over, or we can take the métro two stops to Rihour, which is close to most of the hotels, but if we decide to walk into town we will probably follow the signs to centre ville. This is perhaps a mistake. The route leaves the station on the upper level and plunges us into a modern district with very little French character (the plan was done by a Dutch architect). We have to walk for ten minutes along a windy viaduct to reach the more reassuring architecture of the nineteenth-century quarter, with its neat classical station and busy cafés.

A better route, though it is not signed, involves leaving the station by the ground floor exit and then walking through a little park on the edge of Euralille. The park is somewhat bare, but we soon come to a cobbled lane leading through a splendid seventeenth-century Spanish city gate to a little seventeenth-century square. The gently curved Rue de Roubaix and the short Rue Anatole France, both recently restored, provide an attractive way of approaching the opera house and Grand'Place.

The best time to arrive in Lille, if we can possibly time it, is early on a Friday evening, just as the Lillois are beginning to gather on the Grand'Place. A train leaving London at about 4 pm would do fine. We would then reach the square at the magical twilight time the French call *l'heure bleu*. If it is winter, and the light is beginning to fade, so much the better, as the square looks particularly seductive at this moment, especially in a light drizzle, with the street lamps shining on the smooth paving stones.

III. A weekend in Lille. Lille is the perfect size of town for a weekend break, combining the pleasures of Paris and Brussels in a compact area. We can find almost everything we want within walking distance of our hotel, or we can take the métro to reach the places that are a little further away. There are, admittedly, not too many museums, but then we probably don't want to spend a whole weekend looking at paintings or stuffed birds. It has two very good museums and that is probably enough. The rest of the time is for walking, or buying cheese, or eating lunch, or gasping at the prices of French haute couture, or drinking coffee, or watching the chess players in the Vieille Bourse, or trying to resist the plump waffles sold in Meert.

We can, if we arrive in Lille on a Friday evening, spend an hour before dinner following walk 1, which is very short. Otherwise, this is something for Saturday morning, before we move on to walk 2, which takes us into the old quarters. There is a museum to visit on this walk, but it is quite small, and does not take long, and is utterly charming. Then we might stop for lunch, perhaps in a restaurant on the Rue du Gand, or sitting at a table in a cobbled courtyard somewhere in Vieux Lille.

The centre of Lille gets quite busy on a Saturday afternoon, so walk 3 takes us into a quieter quarter, where we look at the citadel, a harbour and a couple of statues. There may not be much daylight left if we are here in winter, but we might find an hour to squeeze in walk 4, which is very short, no more than an hour.

We now come to Saturday evening, an especially seductive time in Lille when the historic buildings are illuminated and the streets are packed. Lille may be an old industrial town, but it becomes almost Mediterranean at night. Ideally, we will have booked a restaurant well in advance, otherwise we may have problems finding a table.

Lille tends to be quite sleepy on a Sunday morning. We might decide to follow the locals and look around the street market in Wazemmes, but there is also the Palais des Beaux-Arts, described in walk 5, which has two paintings by Goya, several works by Rubens, and an extraordinary collection of seventeenth-century city models. It also has a modern café, where we might sit down to write a couple of postcards.

We can then look for lunch in the neighbourhood, perhaps strolling down to one of the restaurants near the Théâtre Sebastopol. The afternoon could be devoted to walk 6, which takes us through the streets of nineteenth-century Lille, ending up, as everyone inevitably does, on the Grand'Place. Perhaps there is still time left for walk 7, our last in Lille, which takes us to unexpected places near the two railway stations.

Finally, before we leave, we might stop for a beer in Les Trois Brasseurs, a friendly tavern just five minutes' walk from Lille Europe station.

IV. A brief history. Before we begin our walks, we might settle down in one of the cafés on Grand'-Place to read a little about the history of Lille, if only to understand why it seems so different from other French towns. According to a local legend, Lille was founded by a giant-slayer called Lyderic, but we will leave this story until later, and simply mention the more prosaic archaeological theory, which suggests that the town began as a small settlement on an island in the River Deûle. This became known as *l'Isle*, the island.

The settlement is first mentioned in a document signed by the Count of Flanders in 1066. By the thirteenth century, it was, like Bruges and Ghent, one of the great cities of Flanders. When Thomas à Becket fled from England in 1165, he settled here for a time, finding sanctuary in a house in the Rue d'Angleterre.

In the endless wars between the English and the French, Lille tended to take the side of the English, as did other Flemish cities, which led to disaster in 1213 when a French army destroyed much of the town. The reconstruction was carried out by Joanna of Constantinople, Countess of Flanders (seen here on her seal), who founded several hospitals for the poor, including the beautiful Hospice Comtesse we will visit on walk 2.

From the earliest days, Lille has been a city under siege. It suffered three sieges in just seven years between 1297 and 1304. Following the first of these, King Philip the Fair of France captured the town and consolidated his power by constructing an enormous castle with eighteen towers. Five years later, Lille was captured by a Flemish army, but Philip the Fair recovered it in 1304. The town remained reluctantly French up until 1369, when it passed to Philip the Bold, the Duke of Burgundy, following his marriage to Margaret of Flanders.

Lille went through a particularly rich period under Duke Philip the Good, who spent long periods in a palace in the town, stimulating the local economy with his fondness for extravagant clothes, elaborate feasts and ornate gothic buildings. The city became famous for its cloth, sold by merchants on the main square where we are perhaps now sitting. In 1425, the painter Jan van Eyck entered the service of Philip the Good

19

and settled in Lille, probably living at the court. He carried out on various missions, sometimes secret, on behalf of the duke, including an assignment in 1428 when he was sent to Portugal to paint a portrait of Isabella, daughter of the King of Portugal. The portrait was sent back to Philip for his approval; convinced of her beauty, he married her in 1430. The following year, in an attempt to revive the spirit of chivalry, Philip founded the Order of the Golden Fleece, which held its first meeting in the church of St Pierre in Lille.

When Charles the Bold, Philip's son, entered Lille in 1468, he was entertained with various street performances laid on by the city, including one in which three naked women represented the Judgement of Paris. Nine years later, Charles lay dead in a frozen pond outside Nancy, killed while attacking the city. His daughter, Mary of Burgundy, married Maximilian of Austria, and the future of the city became a matter of Hapsburg policy, determined in Vienna and Brussels.

In 1506, the city passed to the Spanish Hapsburgs and remained under Spanish control for 161 years. This led to a further period of prosperity which gave Lille many of its finest buildings, mostly constructed in a vivacious baroque style influenced by Antwerp and Brussels. The old stock exchange (opposite) on

13. « LILLE » La Statue de Napoléon.
(Intérieur de la Bourse).

Edition G. L.

Grand'Place is the most striking building in this Spanish-Flemish style, but there are many other examples in the narrow streets of Vieux Lille, which we explore on walk 2.

The Spanish influence ended in 1667 when Louis XIV captured the city. One of his first projects was to defend Lille with a massive fortress described as the 'queen of citadels' (opposite). It was designed by Vauban, the French military architect entrusted with protecting France's eastern frontier with a string of such fortresses. In addition, several new military buildings were constructed in the town and, in a pompous gesture of absolute power, the massive Porte de Paris was built on the main road from Paris.

Lille rapidly lost its Flemish character at this time, changing from a prosperous Flemish city on the southern edge of the Low Countries to a sombre fortress town in the north-eastern corner of France. Its links with Flemish cities such as Brussels and Ghent were severed, and its merchants had to learn to do business with Parisians instead. The architecture changed, too, as Louis XIV remodelled Lille into an elegant French town. After building his queen of citadels, Vauban was appointed to created a new royal quarter with broad streets laid out on a grid pattern. The houses were built in the sober French baroque of Louis XIV, using stone rather than brick, thus bringing an end to Lille's brightly painted façades.

Despite Vauban's elaborate fortifications, Lille was captured by the Duke of Marlborough in 1708. It was occupied by Dutch troops, but only for five years, until the Treaty of Utrecht restored it to the French. The local population was apparently overjoyed. 'It would take an entire book to describe the welcome that the people have given to the troops of the King,' wrote the Marshal de Montesquiou, who led the French troops into Lille and ended the day completely drunk. 'I was offered so many glasses of wine to drink toasts the king that I could hardly sit on my horse.'

The outbreak of the French Revolution led to considerable upheaval in Lille, but the city escaped the worst excesses of the Terror, and the city's guillotine was apparently never needed. Several new measures, some of them faintly ridiculous, were enacted in an attempt to eradicate the Catholic religion. The Porte Saint-Maurice became the Porte de l'Egalité, the Porte de Fives became the Porte de la Guerre and the Cour du Papegay was renamed the Cour de Geai to avoid anyone being required to utter the distasteful word Pape (Pope).

In 1792, the city had to face another siege, this time by the Austrians. For seven days and nights, the Austrian artillery bombarded the town. Some 30,000 cannon-balls and 6,000 mortar shells fell on the town, destroying 700 buildings, including the ancient Saint-Etienne church on Grand'Place. Yet the town stubbornly refused to surrender. In one famous episode, a barber in the Saint-Sauveur quarter was shaving a customer in his shop when a shell exploded beside him. He snatched up a piece of shrapnel, cried out 'Here is my new shaving dish,' and used it to shave fourteen customers.

The Austrians finally gave up the siege after running low on shells. The National Convention in Paris later praised the citizens of Lille for showing 'their love for liberty and hatred of tyranny'. Amidst the ruins of the Saint-Sauveur quarter, which had borne much of the destruction, a decree was read out, declaring that 'Lille had served its country well'. The artist Louis-Joseph Watteau (a nephew of the famous Watteau) stood in the rubble to record the scene for a painting that now hangs in the Musée Comtesse.

Lille's long history of sieges finally came to an end in the nineteenth century following Napoleon's defeat at Waterloo. The city gradually became transformed into an industrial centre, inspired by the booming

English cities of Manchester and Liverpool. The old Flemish farms around Lille disappeared, replaced by large red brick factories with conspicuous chimneys. The factory owners used their massive wealth to build fanciful mansions in eclectic styles, though few were as eccentric as the one built in the suburb of Tourcoing in 1892. It was designed for Victor Vaissier, a local soap-manufacturer who turned a modest family business into an international company. Vaissier made his fortune manufacturing luxury soaps under the brand name 'les Princes du Congo' which he supplied to the court of Belgium and the Bey of Tunis. He initially instructed an architect to build him a mansion supported on the backs of four elephants, but when that proved just a little too difficult, the soap baron settled on an exotic Oriental palace with a huge stained-glass dome. The building, known as the Palais du Congo, proved ridiculously expensive to maintain and was torn down in 1925, soon after the owner died, leaving just two modest gate lodges on the Rue de Monvaux as a reminder of the folly.

While industrialists indulged their architectural fantasies in the suburbs, many people in the city lived in appalling slums, crowded together in damp houses, and even in dark basement rooms. In his 1853 collection of political verse, *Les Châtiments*,

Victor Hugo condemned these 'Cellars of Lille where people perish under your stone ceilings'. In the same year, a local composer called Alexandre Desrousseaux wrote a beautiful lullaby, *P'tit Quin'quin*, about a poor lacemaker from the Saint-Sauveur quarter who put down her work to sing her child to sleep.

Several decades after Desrousseaux wrote his classic lullaby to send the children of France to sleep, another Lille musician composed a rousing song that would inspire the proletariat to take to the streets. The words of the Internationale were written in 1888, after the fall of the Paris Commune, by a woodworker from Lille called Eugène Pottier. They were set to music by Pierre Degeyter, a musician who lived in the Saint-Sauveur quarter.

By the late nineteenth century, the fortifications built by Vauban had become useless against modern artillery. At the outbreak of the First World War, the French army decided to abandon Lille to the Germans, declaring it an 'open city'. The citadel was

27

emptied of useful war material, including 400 cannons and three million rounds of bullets, and the garrison was evacuated in late August, leaving the town totally undefended. For more than a month, while furious fighting went on nearby, the people of Lille lived an unreal existence, totally uncertain of their future. On 2 September, some German soldiers entered the city and occupied the town hall, but they did not stay. Then a group of German cavalry rode into Lille to ask for directions, but they, too, left the town again.

The French strategy changed dramatically in early October when General Joffre decided that Lille had to be defended at all cost. He sent 4,000 reservists and some cavalry to hold onto the city. There was fighting at Fives, just east of the town, and again in the south, but the French fought off the attackers. Finally, on 11 October, the German army launched a massive artillery bombardment. Over the next two days, more than 5,000 shells fell on the city, destroying over eight hundred buildings. With 70,000 German soldiers poised to attack, the French commander finally decided to surrender. On 12 October, a white flag appeared on the Eglise du Sacré-Coeur and a carrier pigeon flew over the rooftops carrying the message to French headquarters that Lille had fallen.

That lone pigeon was lucky to get out of Lille alive.

Once installed in Lille, the German authorities issued an order to shoot all the pigeons in the city. A sign went up on the railway station renaming it the Haupt-bahnhof and all the clocks were moved to German time. For the next four years, Lille lay just twelve kilo-metres behind the German trenches, occupied by troops in grey uniforms.

The British army finally entered Lille on 17 Octo-ber 1918 without firing a single shot. A newspaper reporter said of Lille that it resembled 'a dead city on the edge of the desert'. The people were starving and many quarters had been reduced to rubble. The socialist mayor, Gustave Delory, almost immediately launched a reconstruction plan, while a few enter-prising shopkeepers began to earn some money selling postcards of the ruins, like the view of the Bourse on the previous page, or this picture of the Vieux Marché aux Poulets, taken in October 1919, less than a year after the war ended, and bought by someone who wrote simply, 'Un bonjour de Lille,' making no mention of the devastation.

The trauma of the war years led the city to construct five large war memorials in the 1920's and 1930's, the largest of them on the site of the Rihour Palace, but the most moving, perhaps, put up near Vauban's citadel to commemorate five members of the resis-

LILLE après le Bombardment. — Rue du Vieux Marché aux Poulets.
Lille after the Bombardment. — « Vieux Marché aux Poulets » Street — LL.

tance executed by the Germans. Postcards of the memorials apparently sold well in the post-war years, judging from the number still found in Lille's second-hand shops.

Lille was occupied again in the Second World War, though this was less of a shock for the Lillois, who had been there before. The city never really recovered after the war, especially after the textile factories were hit by competition from the Far East in the 1960's, forcing them all out of business. The houses in the old centre, many dating from the Spanish period, were left to rot, until finally it seemed as

31

if the only solution was to tear it all down and start again. This was in fact done in the Saint-Sauveur quarter, south of the centre, after a 1954 survey showed that more than half of the dwellings had no running water. The city council demolished the entire neighbourhood, including the house where Desrousseau had composed his lullaby, replacing the old crooked streets with modern apartment buildings set in green spaces.

Elsewhere in Lille, a few people were waking up to the danger. As early as 1964, an organisation called Renaissance du Lille Ancien was set up to save historical buildings in the quarters to the north of the centre. But the real renaissance of Lille began, everyone will tell you, in 1973 when a dynamic socialist called Pierre Mauroy was elected mayor. This in itself was not particularly revolutionary. The city had been a bastion of socialism for more than a century. But Mauroy had a particular passion for Lille which went far beyond party politics, earning him the nickname 'Grand Quin'quin'. One of his first grand projects was to give the city the world's most advanced metro system, with smart stations and fully automatic trains.

The restoration of Vieux Lille only became a priority for Mauroy in the late 1970's. The cynical explanation is that he was shamed into action after a Gaullist politician produced an election poster showing a photograph of the pretty Place des Oignons in about 1900 alongside a view of the same square taken in the 1970's, with all the buildings by then derelict. 'Is this socialism?' the poster asked. Mauroy is said to have immediately launched an ambitious project to restore life to the old cobbled streets.

Mauroy left Lille for several years to serve in the Mitterand government, but returned to local politics as mayor in 1989. Lille was by then a sprawling urban region with more than one million inhabitants. It had a scintillating old quarter, a new business district taking shape, and an ambition to become a major railway hub. The city was eventually so confident that it put in a bid to host the 2004 Olympic Games. The bid failed, but it was rewarded with the title of European capital of culture in 2004.

As we wander along the new viaduct that leads between the old and new railway stations, perhaps feeling vaguely queasy from the slight judder of passing traffic, it is worth remembering that this entire quarter was once a bleak patch of wasteland on the edge of a ring road. Now Lille is booming it is becoming increasingly difficult to remember that this was once a city with no future.

WALK ONE

Grand'Place

From Grand'Place to the Vieille Bourse

I. Grand'Place. Our first walk is not a long one.
We are not going to do much apart from stroll around
the Grand'Place, drink some coffee and look in the
courtyard of the Vieille Bourse. That is, if we are
around when it is open (normally Tuesday to Sunday
2-7 pm). If we arrive at the wrong time, we will have
to return again later, or we risk missing the most
beautiful courtyard in the city.

A coffee, or, if we have arrived later, a drink, might
be the way to begin. There are several good cafés in
the neighbourhood, but the place I have in mind is
Café Méo at 5 Grand'Place, which is open from 8.30
am, serves excellent coffee, and has a window counter
with a perfect view of Grand'Place.

One thing we may already have noticed is that
the name Grand'Place does not appear on any maps
of Lille. We have to hunt out old maps in antiquar-
ian shops to find the square with this name. It is

officially called Place du Général de Gaulle, and marked as such on every map, yet almost no one in Lille refers to it by the proper name. People prefer to call it Grand'Place, or Place de la Déesse (after the statue in the middle of the square), or, occasionally, Place du Furet (the name of a large bookshop here). It is easy to understand why the name Place du Général de Gaulle has never caught on, for this square is very much a Grand'Place, like the great squares of Brussels and Antwerp.

If we have a spot with a view of the square, we

should be able to see the tall column with a statue on top known as La Déesse (The Goddess). The monument was designed by the architect Charles Benvignat to commemorate Lille's resistance to the Austrians in 1792. The statue was put up half a century after the event, revealing the city's enduring pride in its heroic stand against the

Austrians. The column shows the Goddess of Lille –
modelled, some say, on the mayor of Lille's wife –
holding a fuse in her right hand while pointing at the
inscription on the base of the column, which quotes
Mayor André's response to the Austrian ultimatum.
'We are going to repeat our oath of allegiance to the
Nation, to preserve liberty and equality or to die at
our posts. We will not break our word.'

Ninety years after the siege, the people of Lille
celebrated the event once again by unveiling a bust
of Citizen André. Patriotic citizens could pay ten
centimes for a souvenir sheet (reproduced overleaf)
that showed scenes of the siege, including the famous
story of the barber who shaved using a fragment of
shrapnel as a bowl. It also reproduced the Mayor's
scrawled response to the Austrian ultimatum, revealing that he hesitated over the wording before arriving
at the version carved on the stone column.

While we are sitting here, we can look at the Vieille
Bourse on the other side of the square, though we will
have to wait until we are close up to admire the
exuberant decoration. When work began on this
building in 1652, Lille was still governed by the
Spanish. The city magistrates decided to build a stock
exchange in the hope that Lille could become an
important commercial centre, like Antwerp and

Amsterdam. The design was inspired by the old Antwerp exchange, but the building was in fact composed of twenty-four individual houses. The middle house on each side incorporated an impressive Flemish baroque entrance, and was considerably wider than the other five in the row.

The architect, Julien Destrée, had trained as a carpenter and sculptor. And it shows. The building looks like an ornate wooden cabinet covered with elaborate decoration. There are, as we will see later, fierce-looking bearded men, lions' heads, heaps of fruit and sad-eyed women. The four entrances lead into a lovely open courtyard surrounded on all four sides by arcaded galleries. The money dealers were expected to work in an open courtyard, as in the Antwerp exchange, to ensure that God could observe their transactions. Of course, when it rained they could retreat under the arcades and perhaps evade detection.

The Flemish belfry that rises above the houses to the left of the Bourse looks as if it must belong to the town hall. It is in fact attached to the Lille chamber of commerce, an early twentieth-century red brick building designed by Louis Cordonnier to harmonise with the sixteenth-century Bourse. The 76-metre belfry blends in perfectly with the old buildings, but

39

LILLE — Horloge de la Nouvelle Bourse
Grande aiguille, Longueur 2m28
Petite aiguille,   »   1m78
Épaisseur des aiguilles   0m,62s
Poids des deux aiguilles en aluminium
        9 kilogs environ

for the Socialist town council it was an arrogant symbol of capitalist power in the heart of the city. When a new town hall was built in the 1920's, they made sure that its belfry, at 104 metres, was significantly higher than the one on the chamber of commerce. They even added a searchlight on top to prove the point (see the night-time view on p. 141). Yet the new town hall is a long way from the centre, in a quarter that few people visit, whereas the capitalists are bang in the centre. Their belfry also has more charm, with carillon bells chiming French folk tunes on the hour and clock faces with ceramic numerals glinting in the sunlight. The picture shows the hands being installed.

II. Around Grand'Place. It is now time to look at the square. After leaving the café, we turn right to look at a impressive classical building with a double staircase. Known as La Grand-Garde, it was built in 1717 as a guard house, but is now home to the Théâtre du Nord. The tall Flemish building to the left is occupied by *La Voix du Nord*, Lille's daily newspaper. It was built in 1936 in the style of a Flemish step gable house, but at least twice the size using reinforced concrete, which makes it look somewhat ridiculous. The ground floor has been turned into a shopping gallery, but the newspaper still occupies the upper floors and the curious penthouse.

We now head in the direction of the statue of La Déesse, passing a large bookshop, Le Furet du Nord ('The Northern Ferret'), which occupies a row of three houses. Founded in the 1950's as a small local bookstore, it was forced to modernise when a large Fnac multimedia store opened behind La Voix du Nord. The Furet expanded its surface area from 50 to 8,000 square metres, installed rows of cash desks and employed young staff on rollerblades to fetch the books. Locals now like to boast that Le Furet is the biggest bookshop in the world. There is even a plaque to emphasise the point, unveiled by Pierre Mauroy when the new shop was opened in 1992, but one wonders if can possibly be true. A French newspaper recently described it as the largest bookshop in France, which is more like it.

The Hôtel Bellevue stands next to Le Furet. Many famous people have stayed here in the past, though they might now have some difficulty finding the entrance, as it has moved from the square to the Rue Jean Roisin. Our route continues across the Rue Nationale and down the cobbled Rue Esquermoise. This is one of the most seductive streets in Lille, with some beautiful nineteenth-century shops such as Pâtisserie Meert at number 27. A bakery opened on this site in 1761, but Meert's dates from 1839. The extravagant interior was designed by Ben Vignat, who embossed his name and construction date on the solid iron front door. The architect was rightly proud of the fabulous richness of the design, the gilded mirrors, iron balconies, elaborate mouldings and delicate frescos.

The entrance hall is decorated with a few mementos, including photographs of French pastry chefs attending national congresses in 1924 and 1925, and a printed invitation to the opening of the new salon de thé in December 1909. The shop became an official supplier to King Léopold II of the Belgians in 1864 and later included the mother of Charles de Gaulle among its faithful customers. The young Charles was apparently fond of Meert's waffles filled with Madagascar vanilla, clearly one thing to which his response was not the familiar 'Non.'

We continue down this street, past a shop called Nous Savons Tout. But we must not let soap distract us from the literary bookshop L'Arbre à Lettre on the opposite side of the street. The façade is nothing special, but the interior has been expertly restored. It is worth going into the shop, if only to discover a typical Lille architectural style dating from the seventeenth century. We begin inside the main house, but then come to a courtyard, and beyond that a second house. This style, which developed at a time when land within the city walls was scarce, has given Vieux Lille an intriguing warren of narrow alleys and secret courtyards. These had become notorious slums by the 1970's, but have now been superbly restored, almost always as shops, and often (as in this case) with glass roofs built over the former courtyard.

Another building to admire (this time from the outside) is Nos. 83-85, a flamboyant pink baroque confection with splendid iron railings. It is here that

LILLE — Le Nouveau Théâtre

we turn right, following the curved frontage of the Librairie du Verseau, to reach Rue Basse. This is another attractive street where we pass large mansions with coach entrances that sometimes let us see into the courtyard. One of these coach gates on the right-hand side of the street, named Passage Basse-Lepelletier, leads us into an attractive eighteenth-century courtyard. But there is more if we go deeper. We pass through two tiny hidden courtyards, now occupied by attractive restaurants, before finally emerging on the Rue Lepelletier. Here we turn left to reach the little Place du Théâtre, though there is no theatre any more. It burned down in 1903, leaving an empty space where a new opera house was finally built, designed by the same architect as the Bourse de la Commerce, but in a quite different neo-classical style. The work began in 1907 and was almost finished when the photograph opposite was taken, not long before the First World War. The opera house was inaugurated during the German occupation, and again, more correctly, in the 1920's.

III. Vieille Bourse. We are almost at the end of the walk, but we have one last building left to visit. If we stand on the steps of the opera house, we are close to the spot where a photographer took the view over-leaf of the façade of the Vieille Bourse, at a time just after the arrival of the motor car. The building was used as an exchange up until 1920, but it then gradually fell into ruin. It was finally restored in the late 1980's, but the credit for once does not go to Pierre Mauroy. The renovation, which took from 1989 to 1997, was paid for by twenty-three French companies. They were allowed to add their names in the cartouches above the windows, but very discreetly, so that only a few are recognisable, such as the logo

45

of the Crédit Agricole bank above the entrance on Place du Théâtre.

Now we must go inside to look at the courtyard. The arcades were decorated in the nineteenth century with plaques that commemorate famous French scientists, inventors and philosophers. One celebrates Louis Pasteur, who founded the science of microbiology while working at Lille University. Another plaque lists the achievements of Kuhlman, who established a large chemical industry outside Lille.

The courtyard is now occupied by second-hand booksellers who heap banana boxes full of old books along the benches where the stockbrokers once sat. A few people gather here during the week to play chess and, on Sunday afternoons, the bookstands are moved to one side to allow locals to dance the tango.

A statue of Napoleon I was placed in the centre of the courtyard in 1854, as seen in the old photograph on page 21, but it was removed in 1986, leaving just a concrete circle marking the spot. The statue was forgotten for several years, but now occupies a place of honour in the Musée des Beaux-Arts (see page 129).

We might spend a few minutes rummaging through

the racks of second-hand French paperbacks, perhaps picking up a copy of Marguerite Yourcenar's memories of a northern French childhood to read on the train home. Once we are finished, we can perhaps leave by the entrance next to stand number 22. This brings us out on the Rue des Manneliers, opposite the flamboyant rococo shop front of A la Cloche d'Or, a jewellery shop which has hardly changed since the photograph on page 4 was taken.

We end the walk back on Grand'Place, or Place du Général de Gaulle, or whatever name we want to use, perhaps sitting on the edge of the stone fountain, watching the lights come on, waiting for something to happen.

Vieux Lille

From the Place du Théâtre to
Notre-Dame de la Treille

I. Rang de Beauregard. The next walk takes us into the ancient quarter to the north of Grand'Place, down narrow cobbled alleys and into the secret little squares of Vieux Lille. Thirty years ago, this seventeenth-century district had become a slum, but it has been painstakingly restored to its original grandeur. On this walk, we will look inside a medieval hospital, admire the interior of an Art Deco fish shop and pass some splendidly restored buildings, but before we do anything else we should perhaps have a coffee.

The café I have in mind is not far from Grand'Place. It is on the Place du Théâtre, where the city theatre stood until it burned down in 1903. The Chamber of Commerce occupies one side of the square, but it is the opposite side that interests us now. A row of fourteen almost identical houses known as the Rang de Beauregard was built for local cloth merchants in 1686-87, but under the strictest of planning controls. The architects were required to copy the Flemish renaissance style of the Vieille Bourse, though they were allowed to add any decoration they liked.

One of the owners took advantage of this loophole to decorate his house with a sign of a golden windmill. The Moulin d'Or was acquired in 1831 by a local fashion retailer who supplied Lille women with ribbons, lace bonnets and corsets. The shop, Morel et Fils, has survived almost intact, its Empire style shop front one of the few left in Lille. It was until recently a second-hand bookshop, but is now occupied by an art café. We can sit here for a while, admiring the iron columns, wooden staircase and seductive mannequins left behind by the family lingerie business. Then it is time to go.

II. Vieux Lille. Once past the chamber of commerce, we have to look for a corner house, the Maison du Bras d'Or, where a golden hand is attached to an iron balcony. This hand originally hung from a wooden house built on this site in the 1500's, pointing merchants in the direction of the port. The wooden house was demolished in 1767, but the original golden hand was spared. We are thus following a very ancient tradition as we turn down the Rue Grande-Chaussée, which has always been, just as the name suggests, an important route. In the eighteenth century, rich owners built grey sandstone houses with ornate balconies, such as the mansion now occupied by the Laura Ashley shop. In the 1920's, local owners briefly flirted with the Art Deco style we see at Nos. 15 and 17.

The gleaming façade of L'Huîtrière stands at the end of the street. This fishmonger's shop was built in 1926 in a pure Art Deco style. The mosaics on the façade are decorated with pictures of fish swimming around in the sea, or with Lillois discussing the catch (overleaf). We find more maritime mosaics inside the shop, though we will see almost nothing of the famous l'Huîtrière fish restaurant, which is reached through a dark passage on the left.

We now turn right along the Rue des Chats-Bossus, which translates as the Street of the Hunchbacked Cats. We can see a black hunchbacked cat on a former tavern sign above the shop at No. 12, though the street name has nothing whatever to do with cats. It is simply a corruption of the French word *caboche*, a hobnail, which served as the trade sign of the mediaeval guild of tanners.

The street bends slightly to the left, following the outline of a vanished feudal castle, and we arrive at

the tiny Place des Patiniers, hardly a square at all, where a local architect, A. Douchy, designed an inventive corner building at No. 20, adding a little plaque with his name in Art Nouveau letters above the door. Then comes another square, the Place du Lion d'Or, no larger than the previous, where an architect has designed an utterly eccentric building in English mock Tudor style, complete with jettied windows.

We are now in the heart of an old quarter of narrow alleys, dark stone cellars and odd little shops. The little alley at No. 13 bis leads to a workshop where lutes are made. And we should take a good look at the lovely stone house at No. 15, whose ancient stone cellar is partly visible from the street.

Turn right along Rue St Jacques, and left down the Rue des Tours, passing a mansion on the left at No. 7 dated 1692. We are now following the line of a moat that once surrounded the Château de Courtrai. Built in about 1300 by Philip the Fair, the castle was an impressive square fortification decorated with no fewer than eighteen tall round towers. No matter how spectacular it looked, it was seen as a symbol of oppression, and no one objected when it was gradually demolished in the seventeenth century, leaving nothing behind to show where it stood apart from the name of the street we are on.

When we go left down the Rue de la Rapine, we are following one of the streets that stood within the castle walls. It brings us out on another square, Place Louise-de-Bettignies, which looks more like a proper square than the others we have passed. It used to be called Place St Martin, but was renamed after the First World War in honour of a local woman who fought in the resistance. Arrested as a spy, Louise de Bettignies was sentenced to death in 1915, but the sentence was later commuted to imprisonment in Lille's citadel. It hardly made any difference, as Louise died of malnutrition in September 1918. A statue was put up in her honour after the war, but not on the square that bears her name. It is on the Boulevard Carnot, on the road to Roubaix, a bit out of the way for us.

III. The Porte de Gand. We now take a brief detour to the right, down the Rue de Gand, past old houses that have been turned into attractive restaurants. This enormously appealing street leads to the Porte de Gand, a picturesque city gate built in brick during the Spanish period. To make it even more attractive, the upper floor of the gate is now occupied by a restaurant. However, putting thoughts of food to one side for a moment, we walk through the vaulted passage on the left, thus avoiding the traffic, to reach a spectacular series of earthworks added in the seventeenth century by Vauban. This is the perfect spot to gain an impression of the vast system of moats and ramparts designed by Vauban to absorb the impact of artillery shells and trap attacking armies.

We now retrace our steps to Place Louise de Bettignies, where an unusual cabinet-maker's workshop survives at No. 14. It was founded, according to the shop sign, by Camille Stopin, Ebeniste, in 1860. A craftsman continues to work in the basement, restoring old cabinets and chairs, and making modern replica antiques.

A striking building opposite (at No. 23) is decorated with red brick walls and garlands of fruit. Built by Gilles-de-la-Bou, a cloth merchant, in 1636, it is one of the earliest examples of Lille's pleasing variant of the Flemish renaissance style, and inspired the architecture of the Vieille Bourse, built a quarter of a century later. When Gilles-de-la-Bou had this house built, it overlooked a picturesque branch of the River Deûle. Bales of cloth were unloaded on the quayside and lifted into the attic through the row of dormer windows. The picturesque harbour disappeared in 1934 when it was filled in to create the broad Avenue du Peuple Belge. This project robbed the quarter of much of its charm, but even worse was to come in the 1960's when the city decided to tear down the old neo-classical law courts and put up the brutal modern Palais de Justice we see now.

So we turn our backs on the Peuple Belge and walk in the direction of the Hôtel de la Treille. The Rue de la Monnaie, named after a mint once located here, runs to the right. This ancient street has several recently-restored houses from the seventeenth century, including one, No. 8, with a statue of the Virgin in a niche. Further along, a ruined wall on the right, now buried in ivy, is all that remains of a medieval water mill. The arched doorway has a stone carved with the date 1642, though the '16' has almost worn away. Just beyond here, we pass the offices of Renaissance du Lille Ancien at No. 22, the admirable organisation founded in 1964 to save the historic buildings of Vieux Lille from demolition or, almost as bad, aluminium window frames.

IV. Musée de l'Hospice Comtesse. A heavy oak door at No. 32 leads into the Hospice Comtesse, a hospital founded in 1237 by Countess Joanna of Constantinople, daughter of Count Baldwin of Flanders. It is one of the oldest surviving hospitals in Europe, with a vast sick ward similar in style to the

St John Hospital in Bruges. The hospice became an orphanage after the French Revolution, admitting thousands of boys and girls through its forbidding oak doorway. Finally, in 1962, it was turned into a fascinating museum of local history.

The sick ward is an impressive gothic hall of 1468 with a vaulted roof and niches set in the stone walls for the patients to use as bedside tables. A little chapel at the far end is separated from the ward by a rood screen. A plaque in the chapel records the 120 wounded French soldiers who were brought here for treatment after the Battle of Fontenoy in 1745.

The kitchen is a charming Dutch interior, almost like a painting by Vermeer, with painted blue and white tiles on the walls (opposite). But most of the tiles are not Dutch. They were produced in a local porcelain factory which opened after the city fell to Louis XIV and the trade in the genuine Dutch article dropped sharply.

The refectory, next to the kitchen, has a splendid carved wooden fireplace and dark green walls. Then we come to a small wood-panelled room with a collection of eight portraits of dukes and duchesses of Flanders. These were painted in the sixteenth century, long after they were all dead, so we cannot expect much accuracy. We see Philip the Bold, the

duke with the long hooked nose, at the top right, directly above his wife Margaret. The second figure is his son, John the Fearless, who inherited the family nose, and married Margaret of Bavaria, seen below. Then comes Charles the Bold, looking more pensive than bold in this portrait, paired with Isabella of Bourbon, his second wife, and finally Maximilian of Austria, who has somehow been matched up with Isabella of Portugal, wife of Philip the Good.

Other rooms on the ground floor contain desks with secret drawers, apothecary jars, linen chests, and, in the final room, a porcelain mustard pot inscribed 'Royal mustard sold by IBr Delporte, grocer, near the St Andrew's Gate in Lille'. The St Andrew's Gate once stood at the end of the Rue Royale, not far from this museum, but nothing of it has survived.

Now we go up the staircase to reach the former dormitory. This long room contains a fascinating collection of paintings, old shop signs and musical instruments, but the first thing we notice is Guicciardini's *View of Lille*, engraved in the sixteenth century and virtually unrecognisable as the city we have been exploring. Most of the old buildings have gone, not least the extraordinary Château de Courtrai built by Philip the Fair after the capture of Lille in 1297. This castle appears again in a seventeenth-century oil painting on wood, looking here like something out of a fairy tale.

The small bronze figure of Jeanne Maillot we see alongside was a preliminary model for a statue unveiled on the Avenue du Peuple Belge in 1936, just two years after this avenue was created on the site of the old harbour. But who was Jeanne Maillot? Our question is answered, though not entirely, by a seventeenth-century oil painting on the right, which shows the belligerent Jeanne urging the city's archers to drive away the Hurlus. They were Protestant soldiers who roamed this region of the Spanish Netherlands during the sixteenth-century religious wars. The Hurlus reached Lille in 1582, but stopped off in a tavern before attacking the city. Jeanne, who served in the tavern, slipped off to warn the city archers, who launched a surprise attack on the intruders outside the Château de Courtrai.

We now come across some old shop signs rescued from demolished buildings. A large sign painted on six planks of wood once indicated an inn called Au Grand Homme. The 'grand homme' was Napoleon, who is shown leaning against a ruined wall, right hand thrust in his waistcoat, with a castle vaguely visible in the background. Another sign put up by a somewhat unconventional eighteenth-century butcher indicates his trade with a plump figure wearing a Phrygian hat, the Revolutionary symbol of liberty, and a string of sausages around his neck. He once had a clay pipe sticking out of his mouth, but that has disappeared.

Three large views of Lille on the opposite wall show different corners of the city in the eighteenth century. The middle panel shows the Vieille Bourse and the Eglise Saint Etienne (which was destroyed in the Austrian siege), seen from a rustic watermill. The painting on the right illustrates the Eglise Saint Maurice and the Théâtre Lequeux, while the intriguing view on the left shows the impressive dome of the Eglise Sainte Marie Madeleine and the Hospice Général, both still standing, seen from an extraordinary garden with a ravine, bridge and waterfall.

The name Watteau appears on the label, but it is not the famous one. That was Jean-Antoine Watteau, who was born in 1684 in the town of Valenciennes, not far from Lille, but spent almost all of his life in Paris, painting delicate scenes of French courtly life. The three paintings we see here were probably the work of a relative. It could have been one of two Watteaus who worked in Lille, both of them named 'Watteau of Lille'. The older was a nephew, Louis-Joseph Watteau, born in 1731, also in Valenciennes.

His paintings were occasionally in the style of his distinguished uncle, though he also painted historical and religious subjects. This Watteau went to Lille in 1755 to teach at the drawing academy that had opened two years earlier, introducing the students to the art of drawing from the nude. This new approach caused such a scandal that he had to resign and leave town. His son was François Watteau, born in 1758 in Valenciennes. His paintings were more often than not influenced by the frivolous court scenes painted by his famous relative back in the 1710's.

There is a small painting by Louis-Joseph, the father, on the opposite wall. It was painted in 1792, soon after the Austrian siege, when the artist was sixty-one, and illustrates the famous story of Barber Maes, whose shop in the Saint-Sauveur district was destroyed by a shell, but who continued to work in the rubble, shaving fourteen customers using a conveniently-curved fragment of shrapnel as a bowl.

It seems likely that Louis-Joseph was in Lille (or close to the city) during the Austrian bombardment, as another small painting by the elderly artist shows the city being bombarded at night. Louis-Joseph shows the view from the Austrian positions, with mortar shells crashing down on the city, buildings going up in flames and, working away unseen in the

65

smoke, that courageous city barber.

We now find several paintings by the son, François, including a delightful 1802 study of the *Fête du Broquelet*. It shows the procession of the lace-makers held at La Nouvelle Aventure in Wazemmes, a tavern that has long disappeared, though the memory is preserved in the name of a market square. Everyone has come out to this country tavern for the day to join in the drinking, flirting and squabbling. There are several amusing figures in the painting, including an enormous pot-bellied man at the bottom right who seems unable to move from his chair.

François also painted a view of the *Braderie of Lille*, showing the scene outside the Vieille Bourse as people go around selling stockings, fish, oysters, lemons, ducks, hats and vests. Equally fascinating is his painting of the *Procession of Lille*, which shows people marching along carrying long poles with guild emblems on top.

Then we come to two more paintings by Louis-Joseph, dating from 1785, and titled *The Fourteenth Aeronautical Experiment of Blanchard and Lépinard*. The Lillois had already witnessed the ascent of a Mont-golfier balloon two years earlier, but they still turned out in their best clothes to watch the two scientists rise above the city (a habit they kept up, as we see here).

The second painting shows the scene after the aero-nauts had returned to earth somewhere near the Porte de Paris, both looking somewhat exhausted as they are presented to the local aristocracy. In the foreground, a man is already selling a newspaper with details of the adventure.

The museum owns a small sketch of the Battle of Lille of 1708, drawn by an English artist called John Wooten, but done thirty-four years after the event. The sketch, which shows Marlborough preparing to attack the city, was later worked up into a large paint-ing that now hangs in St James's Palace in London.

Opposite, a series of twenty-three portraits depict the Counts and Countesses of Flanders, all painted on wood in the seventeenth-century by Arnould de Vuez. It would take far too long to name them all, though it is perhaps interesting to know that the final portrait shows Mary of Burgundy, who died while she was pregnant after falling from her horse.

It is now time to leave the museum. We turn right along Rue de la Monnaie, past some attractively restored renaissance houses. Those on the right side, beyond the Rue Comtesse, stand on the site of the Palais de la Salle. Nothing remains of this medieval palace, not even a street name. We do not even know its appearance. All that is certain is that here, on 17

February 1454, Philip the Good organised an extravagant banquet known as the Feast of the Pheasant. Planned months in advance by a committee of nobles, the banquet went on for several days and featured some extraordinary decorations. There was a church on top of an elephant, a ship with full rigging, a meadow with fountains and rocks, a castle with a fairy on top, a forest in which wild beasts prowled and, most bizarre of all, an orchestra of twenty-eight musicians placed inside a pie. During the feast, Philip and his nobles vowed to set off on a Crusade against the Turks but, predictably, they failed to keep their word. In the same year, Philip began work on a new gothic palace on land to the south of the Grand'-Place, and the old palace was gradually abandoned.

A coach gate opposite, at No. 61, leads into the courtyard of La Cour des Grands, an eighteenth-century mansion with a row of stables on the right. An elegant restaurant occupies the mansion, though it looked closed when I last passed. We turn left down the next street, the Rue de Peterinck, an appealing cobbled lane where we can see the backs of the stables. The house at No. 8 is occupied by an artist and next door is an Italian delicatessen called La Bottega whose owner caused a minor frisson in 2000 when he published a calendar illustrated with nude

69

photographs of twelve male shopkeepers in the Vieux Lille Quarter. It was very tasteful, as the photographs in the window (and the one opposite) reveal, and proved a huge success. He is now on his fifth edition, but promises that this will be the last.

We now head for the Place aux Oignons. The name has nothing to do with the vegetable, but derives from the donjon that once stood near here. Looking at the flourishing window boxes on No. 2, and the elegant boutiques, it is impossible to believe that this was a slum neighbourhood up until the early 1970's. Goaded into action by an election poster showing the deplorable state of the square, the mayor restored the seventeenth-century houses to their original splendour, revealing hidden details such as the stone carved with the date 1680.

We continue down the Rue des Vieux-Murs, whose modest workers' houses have become popular with artists and craftsmen. On reaching the Rue des Trois Mollettes, we turn left to reach an eccentric church, which began as a neo-gothic building but ended with a distinctly modern look. We may want to sit down inside to read the whole story.

V. Notre-Dame de la Treille. The church of Notre-Dame de la Treille (Our Lady of the Pergola) is named after a medieval statue of the Virgin covered with an iron pergola that originally stood in the collegiate church of Saint Pierre. The statue became a pilgrimage site after a series of miracles happened in front of it in 1254. Sixteen years later, Countess Margaret of Flanders decided to organise a solemn procession around the town walls in honour of Notre-Dame. The procession became an increasingly sumptuous annual event, involving, by the fifteenth century, Biblical scenes and even comedy acts.

The church of Saint Pierre, which stood in the Rue de la Monnaie, was the setting for a splendid ceremony in 1431, when Philip the Good, duke of Burgundy (left), held the first meeting of the Order of the Golden Fleece. The order was founded in an attempt to revive the early medieval ideals of chivalry, but its meetings are remembered only for the gargantuan feasts that lasted for several days.

Saint Pierre was demolished after the French Revolution, but the statue was hidden and later displayed in the church of Sainte Catherine. In the mid-nine-teenth century, some 52 prominent citizens founded a limited company to construct a new church devoted to Our Lady of the Pergola. The foundation stone was laid in 1854, exactly six hundred years after the miracles. We can see a scale model of the planned church in the south transept, which demonstrates the ambitious scale of the project, including twin gothic towers at the west end. These were never begun. The construction dragged on for decades because of funding problems. It took until 1897 merely to build the chapel and apse at the east end, which contain some quaint neo-gothic chapels from this period, including one of 1909 dedicated to Joan of Arc and containing a miniature castle like a toy from a Victorian childhood. Travelling to Paris to view an exhibition of Flemish Primitives, the Belgian writer Joris Karl Huysmans was persuaded to take a look at the unfinished cathedral. 'A deceit, in a worthless town,' he jotted down in his notebook.

Morale was briefly restored in 1913 when the city became a bishopric, and the unfinished church became Lille's Cathedral. By the 1920's, the architects had begun to work with concrete rather than brick, but the project came to a halt again in 1947. The workmen returned in 1953, but only after the authorities had agreed on a much simpler and less costly design. For the next forty years, it seemed to local people that the church would never be completed, and the west end remained closed off with a temporary wall. But finally, just a few days before the end of the century, on 19 December 1999, the new west front was unveiled.

The result is a stark modern design with a wall of marble slabs supported on a steel frame. The marble looks white from the outside, but has a strong ochre tint when seen from the inside. A large stained glass window at the top designed by Ladislas Kijno represents the Resurrection.

The bronze doors at the west end were made by Georges Jeanclos, a French artist born in Paris in 1933, who died before the doors were installed. They are an extraordinary modern work, almost on the scale of the baptistery doors of Florence cathedral. The figure of Our Lady of the Pergola sits at the top of the Tree of Life, holding a bunch of grapes and surrounded by a trellis entwined with vines. Only later do we notice the tiny figures of children on the trellis. Looking more closely, we begin to discover disturbing details, such as the young girl on the right door, near the middle, who is holding a sleeping boy in her arms. The pose recalls Michelangelo's *Pietà*,

suggesting that the boy might be dead. The meaning of the doors becomes painfully clear once we learn that the artist spent his childhood in a concentration camp.

The church stands on the site of the Motte Madame, a moat and bailey castle built by the Counts of Flanders. The scale model of Lille made in the eighteenth century and now in the Palais des Beaux-Arts gives us an impression of the hill when it was planted with trees and skirted by a canal (opposite). The canal has long gone, but if we walk behind the church we can still see the wooden bridges that once crossed the water.

We now go back to the square in front of the church and continue down the cobbled Rue Masurel opposite. A shop on the right sells musical instruments, while Marie Couture opposite displays exclusive wedding dresses in two eighteenth-century interiors. The street becomes even more seductive beyond the bend. Most of the shops are expensive boutiques, but an old bakery has survived on the corner of Rue Lepelletier. It is a branch of Paul, so perhaps it is less authentic than it looks. We can now either continue down Rue Lepelletier to reach Grand'-Place or, if we prefer to explore further, turn left along Rue Basse to return to the Rue des Chats-Bossus. On reaching the little Place du Lion d'Or, we go right to reach the Place des Patiniers, then turn down the Rue de la Clef, a narrow street with little shops selling computer games, alternative fashion and long-playing records. Our walk ends back on the Place du Théâtre.

Medieval Lille
From the Place Rihour to
Eglise St Maurice

I. The Palais Rihour. This is the shortest walk we will do in Lille, as the medieval town has all but disappeared. We will sit in a café, explore the remains of a gothic palace and look inside one church. That is all. I suggest that we begin with a coffee in the Pain Quotidien bakery at 3 Rue de la Vieille Comédie, not far from Grand'Place. We reach it down the Rue du Palais Rihour, a street lined with cheerful seventeenth-century houses built of red brick and white stone. Before entering the café, we should look up at the plaque above the door, now so worn that it is difficult to read much more than the word 'Voltaire'. When it was not so decayed, this tablet recalled the fact that Voltaire's play *Mahomet* was first performed in 1741 in a theatre on this site.

   Now we have a choice. If it is a sunny day we

might want to sit out on the little terrace shaded by white parasols, next to a mechanical roundabout called Le P'tit Quin'quin. Otherwise, we will have to go inside, and perhaps, if we are fortunate, find a table close to a window. Once installed, we can order a coffee, asking for a café crème if we want it served with milk, and read about the gothic palace that once stood here.

The Palais Rihour was begun in 1453 by Philip the Good, duke of Burgundy, to replace the old ducal palace near the Hospice Comtesse. The vast brick palace was decorated in flamboyant late gothic style, and adorned with turrets and gables. All of which took time to build. When Philip moved into his new apartments here in 1463, the building had only reached the second floor, and the noise of masons must have been a constant irritation. The building was finally completed in 1473, too late for Philip, who had died six years earlier, so it was his son, Charles the Bold, who saw the final result. The old engraving opposite shows a building with four wings surrounding a central courtyard, barred windows on the ground floor, a chapel and a curiously modest entrance.

Many famous guests stayed here, including Henry VIII of England in 1513, and Louis XIV in 1667, by which time the palace had become the town hall,

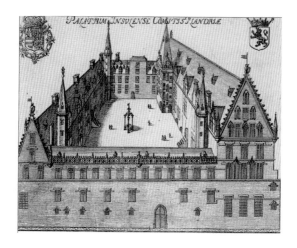

having been sold by King Philip IV of Spain in 1664 to raise money. It was still being used as a town hall in the summer of 1846 when a curious concert was conducted here by Hector Berlioz. He had been commissioned to write a cantata to celebrate the opening of the railway line between Lille and Paris, an event of considerable importance to the northern town, as we will find out on walk 7. Not long after Berlioz appeared here, the gothic palace was demolished and rebuilt the town hall in a gloomy neo-classical style. The work took almost as long as the original palace, from 1846 to 1859, and spared only the late gothic chapel, the guard room and the elegant staircase of honour, which was dismantled and moved to its present location in 1857.

The palace was still standing when the German army occupied Lille in the First World War, but it was destroyed by an accidental fire on Easter Sunday 1916, wiping out a valuable collection of books owned by the city library, and leaving just the staircase and the chapel standing. A new town hall was built on a site in the Saint-Sauveur quarter in 1924-28, and the charred ruins of the old ducal palace were cleared to create the square we see here.

II. A war memorial. The city then made an extra-ordinary decision. In 1924, they approved a plan to build an enormous stone war memorial on the side of the old gothic chapel, facing the Grand'Place. It is a striking monument, designed by the architect J. Alleman, but the location is simply awful. It is decorated with three reliefs by the sculptor E. Boutry, the lowest, *Les Captifs*, showing male prisoners being led off to labour camps while their wives comfort one another. The middle panel, *La Relève*, depicts soldiers wounded in a battle, while the top relief, *La Paix*, illustrates the figure of peace handing a laurel wreath to a soldier. While some local people protested at the site, others who had strong nationalist opinions grumbled about the decision to use the pacifist phrase 'morts pour la paix' rather than the more common 'morts pour la patrie'. During the German Occupation, the nationalists seized the opportunity to replace 'paix' with 'patrie', but the original version was restored after the Liberation.

It is time to take a look at the relics of the palace. But first we should stand on the square in front of the war memorial to read the inscriptions on the paving stones. Some of them are inscribed with the names of sponsors, among them the unexpected Mutual Association of Hairdressers of Lille.

We now go through the brick arch to the left of the war memorial. The wall, now overgrown with ivy, is all that survives of the nineteenth-century town hall. Once through the arch, we will see a computer screen offering information on Lille. It is probably broken, but no matter. We are now outside the tourist office, which has all the information we need. It occupies the former guard room of the ducal palace, an impressive gothic space with a roof supported on three octagonal columns.

Once outside again, we will discover another door on the left. One of the faded gothic inscriptions above

the door reads 'Musée Archéologique.' The other panel is illegible. The museum closed down years ago, but we can, if we are here at the right time of year (April to October), climb the spiral stone staircase to visit the former chapel, now known as the Salle du Conclave. A dark passage at the top of the stairs leads into a lofty gothic interior with a black and white tiled floor. The chapel was used for a time for city council meetings, hence its name. Later, it was occupied by the archaeology museum, which owned a miscellaneous collection of furniture, altarpieces and globes. High above the door, we can see the former rose window, which is now bricked up. A door on the left leads into the duke's private chapel, which has stained glass windows rescued from churches in the region.

Back on the square, we can stand on the spot where the photograph on page 78 was taken about a century ago. It shows the great stone staircase on the right and an elegant octagonal stair tower built of brick. From here we retrace our steps to Pain Quotidien and turn down the Rue de la Vieille Comédie to reach the busy Rue de Béthune. Here we turn left to reach the Eglise Saint Maurice, which is a partly medieval hall church, with five aisles of equal height, though the west front was added in 1855. The exterior was recently restored, revealing intricate details of medieval stonemasonry.

Gate of
Aids

The Citadel Quarter
From Place du Théâtre to the Citadel

I. Place du Théâtre. This is a walk that takes us away from the crowded streets of Vieux Lille into a quarter that has kept much of its provincial charm. We stand in front of the Citadel (opposite), wander through a romantic park and pause before a curious statue inspired by a local lullaby. The walk takes about three hours, but longer if we decide to spend time in the park.

First a coffee. We will find a little Art Nouveau café called Le Carnot that has barely changed since the photograph overleaf was taken around 1900. It is located just behind the Bourse de la Commerce in a strange tall building that occupies the angle between the Boulevard Carnot and the Rue de la Clef. The name of the architect, A. Lemay, appears on a stone on the side facing the boulevard. The developer has

LILLE — Entrée du Boulevard Carnot
Terminus Tramway Mongy-Lille-Roubaix-Tourcoing

also added his name to the building, perhaps in the hope of attracting clients. The interior is very French, with tall mirrors and Art Nouveau tiles. If we are here at a quiet time of day, we might be able to sit at the round table in the corner, which looks out on the opera house, the chamber of commerce and the ornate street lamps on Boulevard Carnot.

We begin the walk outside the Bourse de la Commerce and head down the Rue Lepelletier, a narrow street that we perhaps know quite well by now. On reaching the Rue Basse, we turn left, briefly retracing the route of walk 1, then right along Rue

Esquermoise, passing a mysterious Freemasons' Lodge on the corner of Rue Thiers, on the left. The side wall is decorated with a classical arcade, frieze and, adding to the mystery, a large bas relief showing a pyramid and sphinx.

The Boulangerie Leroy on the right side of the street was established in 1944, according to the painted sign, but probably on the site of a much older bakery. The owner has displayed a page from an old guide to Lille in the window, in which the author describes a bakery founded here in 1686. It was 'famous for its Carrés de Lille praised by Desrousseaux,' the guide says. We will meet Desrousseaux at the end of this walk, so perhaps we should pick up a packet of the large square biscuits he liked.

We soon reach a small square where an old iron road sign gives the distance to Armentières with unusual precision (14.9 kilometres, it says). We take the other road, the Rue Royale, an elegant street lined with nineteenth-century mansions, but leave it shortly to turn left down Terrasse Sainte Catherine. This quiet lane leads to the appealing Sainte Catherine church, a gothic building with a squat stone tower and a baroque gable added in 1727. A tourist information sign opposite the church entrance gives us a brief history of the building and urges us to look inside, promising us a remarkable tabernacle, pine vaulting and a 1687 organ. We would love to do just that, but the church is only open to visitors on Sundays, and even then only for a quarter of an hour before Mass begins.

So unless we are here at the right moment, the church will be locked and we will have to continue on our way through Place Jacques Louchart, a lovely forgotten square popular with artists and students. Then we go right down Rue de la Barre, the old road to Armentières. The street has some handsome eighteenth-century mansions, but we may well be tempted by a little lane on the left called Rue de la Halloterie. It looks irresistible, so we turn down here, passing neat eighteenth-century houses that were once, believe it or not, occupied by brothels. The far end of the street is less interesting, and so we turn right down Rue de la Baignerie and again right down Rue du Quai. This brings us out on the Quai du Wault, a cobbled quayside dating back to the fifteenth century. The little port was built here by John the Fearless, but no longer serves any useful purpose. Maybe that will change, and waterfront café terraces will soon appear, now that the quay has been restored as an urban promenade.

98. LILLE — Quai de Wault

We turn right along the quay, passing a hotel that occupies a former Franciscan monastery. Built from 1622 to 1688 in Lille's attractive baroque style, the convent was barely one hundred years old when the French Revolution broke out, leading to the abolition of the order. Most of the buildings were torn down, leaving just the cloister, which was used by the military before being turned into a hotel.

The quay ends at a busy road where we have to cross to the other side. We then turn left under the chestnut trees to look at a striking stone memorial to the Martyrs of Lille. Carved by the sculptor Félix

Desruelles, it commemorates five members of the resistance executed by the Germans on 22 September 1915. This old postcard shows the memorial soon after it was completed, when tulips grew in front of the monument. The sculptor shows four of the men standing against a wall of the old citadel just before their execution, while a fifth companion already lies dead on the grass. The man on the left is Georges Maertens, a local businessman wearing what looks like his best suit. The next figure is Ernest Deceuninck, an army officer, then Sylvère Verhulst, a worker, and, finally, Eugène Jacquet, a wine

merchant. The victim lying on the ground was eigh-
teen-year-old Léon Trulin.

The Germans arrested Eugène Jacquet for conceal-
ing secret military information in a local café. He was
also found guilty of hiding French soldiers in Lille and
helping a British pilot to escape. The monument was
built after a competition was held in 1924. It was
dynamited by the Nazis in 1940, but restored in the
1960's using the original plaster model.

Another monument stands on the far side of the
small road behind us. Two stone slabs commemorate
Charles de Gaulle, who was born in Lille, not far from
where we are standing, in 1890. 'Fate has never
betrayed a united France,' it reads. A more curious
monument from the First World War stands on the
other side of the canal, on the edge of the Champs de
Mars. The 'Monument Au Pigeon Voyageur' is a
touching memorial to the pigeons that carried
messages during the First World War. Designed by
J. Alleman and R. Aillerie, it shows a woman releas-
ing birds into the sky, while a slain snake lies curled
at her feet. The bas relief on the left side depicts a
pigeon being released in the trenches, while the one
opposite shows a lone bird flying over two dead
soldiers. But this is not simply a memorial to homing
pigeons. An inscription on the right side records that

it is in memory of 'Pigeon fanciers who died for France, executed by the enemy for keeping pigeons.'

II. The Citadel. The cobbled lane to the right leads us through the outer defences of Lille's citadel. We can walk down the lane, pass through a seventeenth-century gate, cross a dry moat and stand in front of the impressive royal gate, seen in this old postcard dating from shortly before the First World War. But we cannot go any further. The citadel is still occupied by the French army, and can only be entered on guided visits organised by the tourist office. So let us sit on the wall outside the gate to read the history of one of the strongest fortresses in France.

The citadel was begun by the military architect Sébastien Le Prestre de Vauban as a key element in his plan to fortify the north-east frontier of France. He proposed to defend the kingdom of Louis XIV with a line of thirty-three citadels running from the North Sea to the Rhine. Vauban drew up the plans for Lille citadel just two months after Louis XIV marched into the city in 1667. Some 5,000 workers were employed on the project, which took three years to complete and used sixteen million bricks and three million sandstone blocks. The stone was transported from quarries at Lezennes, south-east of the city, at

a rate of 2,000 blocks a day.

From where we are sitting, we can only see a very small part of Vauban's elaborate plan, which is based on a five-pointed star surrounded by a complex system of ditches and bastions, with four-metre thick walls to absorb the impact of artillery shells (see the engraving on page 22). An attacking army would have had to breach the outer line of defences, which we passed through, then attack the brick walls from inside the moat. But Vauban made that virtually impossible by making sure that each wall could be protected by guns fired from the opposite flank. So if troops tried to attack the wall on our left, they would be fired on by troops lined up on the wall on our right. (The slightly vertigo inducing detail on page 86 shows how the system worked.)

An eighteenth-century French writer described the citadel as 'the most beautiful fortress ever built in Europe.' We will have to take his word for it, for most of the complex is hidden behind the walls. But the Porte Royale in front of us is certainly impressive. Designed in baroque style with the assistance of the Lille architect Simon Vollant, the monumental Doric gate is decorated with military symbols, three fleurs-de-lys and, at the top, a gilded sun shining through the clouds. Louvois, Louis XIV's secretary of state for war, considered it excessively ornate. 'His Majesty is working on too many buildings to allow the construction of beautiful gates which look good but achieve nothing,' grumbled the military man.

The plaque at the top of the gate tells us that we are standing outside the Boufflers quarter of the citadel. The Marshal de Boufflers was a distinguished soldier in the army of Louis XIV; he took part in the siege of Lille in 1667, led French troops at the Battle of Fleurus, and fought in the sieges of Liège and Namur. He faced a final test in 1708 when the Duke of Marlborough attacked Lille. Despite his advanced age, Boufflers was entrusted with defending the city. The city magistrates, fearing the destruction of Lille, called on him to surrender. He agreed to withdrew his troops to the citadel, where they held out for just forty days.

A nature trail signed 'circuit des remparts' runs around the outside of the citadel walls for two kilometres. We can follow this to discover the rare birds and plants that flourish below Vauban's brick walls. But that is perhaps for another day.

III. Bois de Boulogne. The cobbled lane takes us back to the pigeon monument, where an avenue on the right leads into the Bois de Boulogne. This park was created in the nineteenth century on wasteland outside the citadel, and modelled, as the name suggests, on the famous park outside Paris. Children can ride on a miniature train that runs through a landscape dotted with sheep, visit a small zoo or pick up a handful of tickets to go on fairground rides. There is also a café with tables set out under the chestnut trees.

A second park, the Jardin Vauban, lies on the other side of the canal. This romantic retreat on the edge of the nineteenth-century town was designed in 1865 by Jean-Pierre Barillet-Deschamps, the head gardener of Paris. It has a pleasing artificial feel, with a grotto, waterfalls and a rustic cottage once occupied by the goat-keeper but now home to a puppet theatre. We walk through this park and leave by a gate in the far corner, near the grotto, emerging on the Rue Solférino, an elegant nineteenth-century street that cuts a straight route through the southern quarters.

IV. Palais Rameau. A short distance down the Rue Solférino, we come to the Palais Rameau, an exotic mansion with little Moorish turrets and an impressive octagonal dome. Built in 1878 for Charles Rameau, a local horticulturist, the building incorporates a large greenhouse originally used for horticultural exhibitions. Rameau bequeathed his palace to the city, but insisted that it had to be used for agricultural exhibitions and flower shows. And he added one final demand. The city had to agree to maintain his tomb in the Cimetière du Sud, and to plant it with a potato plant, a vine, strawberries, dahlias and roses.

We now walk past the front of the Palais Rameau and turn right down the street just beyond. Then we go left down Rue de Bourgogne and cross the Rue de la Liberté, a grand nineteenth-century boulevard planted with plane trees. The final stretch of Rue de Bourgogne ends at a dusty little park, the Square Dutilleul. Turning right here we come to the Square Foch, where Marshal Foch sits on horseback at the top of an enormous stone plinth. If we sit on one of the benches to the right, we can read the speech he made to his troops on 12 November 1918 at the end of the war. 'You have won the greatest battle in history and saved the most sacred cause: the liberty of the world. Be proud.'

The monument was designed, once again, by J. Alleman, who had served in the French infantry for four years, fighting at Verdun and the Somme. Despite an unfortunate name (a bit too close to Allemagne), he received several commissions for war memorials, including the monument on Place Rihour we saw on walk 3. His monument to Foch was the last

99

of the large First World War memorials built in Lille and was completed in 1936, just three years before another war broke out.

V. P'tit Quin'quin. Now for the most delightful statue in Lille. A romantic Art Nouveau work at the far end of the park commemorates Alexandre Desrousseaux, the local composer who praised the biscuits sold in the Rue Esquermoise. Desrousseaux charmed nineteenth-century France with a song, composed in 1853, about a poor lace maker from the Saint Sauveur quarter of Lille. The statue, carved in 1902 by Eugène Dépléchin, shows the young mother, who had put down her lace-making tools, holding her sleeping child. The cradle beside her contains a little hand puppet. The bust at the top shows the composer looking slightly alarmed, as if he anticipated the horrendous modern building, now abandoned, that would one day be erected opposite the park.

We can turn left along Rue Nationale to return to Grand'Place, or we can take a slightly longer, but perhaps more interesting route along a parallel street. To take the longer route, which is not that easy to find, we have to turn left along the side of the park, then go right just beyond number 4, through a passage named Rue du Vert Bois. There is no sign

of any 'vert bois' (green forest), and indeed nothing of interest, until we are beyond the café St Germain-des-Prés. But then we come to a house signed 'Horace Pouillet 1910' at No. 2, which has an attractive Art Nouveau window, green glazed bricks, a stained glass stair window and iron brackets that could almost be the work of Charles Rennie Macintosh.

This is not the only hint of sophisticated taste in the neighbourhood. After crossing the Rue de l'Hôpital Militaire (where we can spot the familiar tower of St Catherine on the left) we continue down Rue Saint-Etienne, passing first a clockmaker and then, at number 61, a tall house with a slight hint of the geometrical Vienna Secessionist style.

We continue past a hair-dressing college, where students occasionally spill out onto the street carrying mannequin heads to practise on at home. The street leads into a small square with a modern round building occupied by the Nouveau Siècle. Named after a popular eighteenth-century tavern which once stood here, the building contains a concert hall where the Lille national orchestra performs. The architecture is interesting, but somehow disturbs the eighteenth-century provincial harmony of the houses on the south side of the square.

We are now nearly at the end of the walk, but there is one short stretch of Rue Saint-Etienne still to see, just beyond the Rue du Pas. It is an attractive cobbled lane that leads past the Hôtel Beaurepaire at No. 6, a rare example of French renaissance architecture in Lille. Built as a refuge by the Knights Templar in 1572, the façade is crammed with arabesques, rosaries and candelabra columns. Once across Rue Esquermoise, we can continue along the Rue du Curé Saint-Etienne and turn right down the Rue des Débris Saint-Etienne, which takes its name from the rubble left behind after the destruction of a church on Grand'Place in 1792. Then we go through a passage and are back on the main square.

The Palais des Beaux-Arts

From Grand'Place to the Théâtre Sebastopol

The aim of this walk is to visit the second most important art museum in France without wearing ourselves out too much. Grandly named the Palais des Beaux-Arts, it contains an extraordinary collection of treasures – more than we might expect in a French provincial museum. The highlights include two paintings by Goya, an extraordinary wax head, a bronze statue of Napoleon I, a relief by Donatello, a medieval baptismal font, a painting by Pieter Codde called *Melancholy*, Camille Claudel's bust of her sister, and a room of seventeenth-century scale models of fortified towns. We need to allow at least three hours to see it all, perhaps even longer.

The walk begins on Grand'Place, where we might stop for coffee in Paul at 8 Rue de Paris. This Lille bakery occupies a splendid renaissance house designed in the same style as the Vieille Bourse opposite. The tea room is a warren of intimate Flemish rooms with beams, antique sculptures, decorated tiles and Flemish chairs. There are various breakfast options, but most locals choose Le Complet before turning to the news in La Voix du Nord. A waitress wearing a white baker's hat will return with a grand café crème, a glass of freshly-squeezed orange juice and one of Paul's demi-flûte (a little baguette) to spread with butter and jam.

The sign above the door says 'fondée en 1889', but the bakery here is a more recent arrival. It belongs to a successful French chain that has its origins in the late nineteenth century. The original 1889 bakery was founded by the impressively-named Charlemagne Mayot in the village of Croix, just outside Lille. His grand-daughter Suzanne and her husband carried on the family tradition in Lille, acquiring a bakery called Paul in the Place de Strasbourg. The business expanded rapidly in the 1960's, with branches opening in Paris, London, Turkey and Japan. There are now about 300 outlets of Paul throughout the world, but they almost all manage to retain something of the charm of a traditional French provincial bakery, even the branch on the A1 motorway.

I. The Rue de Béthune. On leaving Paul, perhaps with a small croissant in our pocket for later, we go down the Rue de Paris, then right down the Rue du Sec Arembault. This leads to the Rue de Béthune, a street heavily damaged in the First World War and rebuilt in the 1920's in Art Deco style. The apartment building with floral decoration at Nos. 41-43 is signed by the architect Albert Buhrer and dated 1926. Further on, the two corner buildings at Nos. 55 and 61 are signed by A. Lemay, who also designed the corner building occupied by Le Carnot where we perhaps had coffee at the start of walk 4.

We soon come to the little Place de Béthune, an attractive square with some trees, several likeable cafés and a dilapidated cast iron fountain that still manages to produce a trickle of water. The buildings are in several styles, ranging from the angular modernism of the apartment block at No. 11 to the traditional Flemish gable above La Taverne. A row of more modest seventeenth-century houses has survived on the little Place du Vieux Marché aux Chevaux, just to the left.

Our route continues down Rue de Béthune to another square, this one more French in style. The Place Richebé has a little formal garden in the middle and a splendid statue of General Faidherbe, one of the city's heroes, who fought in the war of 1870 and founded the port of Dakar. The statue, paid for by public subscription, looks like a conventional figure on horseback, except, that is, for the two adoring woman at his feet. One is writing in a book, perhaps recording his victories, but the other, slightly absurd figure, is dressed in armour, a lion's skin and a crown. Now we cross the vast Place de la République, pausing in the middle, above a sunken amphitheatre, to admire the Préfecture du Nord on the right, built in 1865 in the elegant neoclassical style of Napoléon III and decorated with ornate iron railings and a neat little clock.

II. The picture gallery. The Palais des Beaux-Arts stands opposite. It was completed in 1892, after twenty years of work, in a typically pompous late nineteenth-century style, with an extravagance of columns, domes, pointed roofs and vases. The building contains a large collection founded by Napoleon in 1801 and subsequently enlarged by donations, which up until then had hung in the old town hall. It includes works from most European schools, but its strength lies in its Flemish and Dutch sections, especially its Flemish baroque art.

It is a matter of some local pride that this is the

second largest museum in France, surpassed only by the Louvre. It is not just a museum, but a *palace* of fine art. Yet the original design was for a building twice this size. The architect finally had to trim the plan for financial reasons. However, even the smaller version is likely to be quite large enough for most of us. Let us take a look inside.

It is quite an intimidating museum, reached across a vast empty square, entered through a massive hall. Yet it used to be much worse. The museum was closed down for a six-year-long renovation in the 1990's, allowing the interior to be totally redesigned by two architects, Jean-Marc Ibos and Myrto Vitart, who had worked with Jean Nouvel in Paris. They removed the clutter, ripped out an ugly staircase, brought in daylight and, most striking of all, added a new administrative building at the back with a glass curtain wall covered in a pattern of tiny mirrors.

The entrance hall, which used to be crowded with statues, is now entirely empty, apart from Gaetano Pesce's two enormous lamps of glass fragments, hung from the ceiling at either end of the hall like chemistry experiments gone wrong. The main collection of paintings is one floor up, reached by a grand staircase lit by tall stained glass windows. Rubens' *The Descent from the Cross* is the first thing we see, hanging

against a blood red wall that picks up the colour of Mary Magdalene's dress. Rubens based it on a work of 1612, painted soon after his return from Rome, which now hangs in Antwerp Cathedral. The version we see here (and opposite) was commissioned in 1615 for the high altar of the Capuchin chapel in Lille.

Another work by Rubens hangs in this room. The *Martyrdom of St Catherine* altarpiece was painted for the little Saint Catherine church in Lille in the same year as the *Descent from the Cross*, probably during the same visit. It shows Catherine on the steps of a Roman temple, just about to be taken off for execution, looking dreadfully pale and frightened. But, as usual in Rubens, there is too much going on to concentrate on the central drama. He could have cut out some of the cherubs, most of the weapons and that irritating little dog at Catherine's feet.

Anthony Van Dyck's *Christ on the Cross* is far more focused on its subject. Painted in Antwerp in about 1628, not long before he moved to England, it contains a hint of Rubens in the vivid red of the cloak and the yellow of the silk dress. But Van Dyck has set the Crucifixion against a ferocious sky filled with dark storm clouds. Rubens would not have been able to resist adding angelic and canine extras.

Another Antwerp artist, Jacob Jordaens, is repre-

111

sented by a strange little painting titled *Five Studies of Cows.* These five cows were originally preliminary studies for several large works that called for bovine content, but Jordaens' rough work became admired as a painting in its own right, and inspired, as we will find out later, one of Van Gogh's last paintings.

The three panels of the *Triptych of St Peter of Verona* by Jeremias Mittendorff were only recently reconstructed, following the discovery in Paris of the two side wings. The central panel illustrates the thirteenth-century martyrdom of St Peter, while the side panels show episodes from the life of this obscure saint. Almost nothing is known of the artist, except that he worked for a time in the Ypres area.

The next room has some curious Mannerist paintings including a *Vanity* by Jan Sanders van Hemessen. This recent acquisition shows an angel with butterfly wings holding a round mirror with a skull reflected in it. The curators have concluded that there was originally a second panel on the right, probably a portrait of a person receiving proof of their mortality in the form of a skull. 'Ecce rapinam rerum omnium,' we read on the mirror. Behold the pillage of all things. A similar morbid philosophy appears on the back of Barthel Bruyn's *Portrait of a Man.* The original panel has been cut in half so that we can see the trompe l'oeil niche on the back, which contains a skull and bone.

The *Portrait of a Man* by Dirk Jacobsz. also hangs in this room. So does the portrait of his wife, but the couple are separated, for some reason, by a strange *Imaginary View of the Colosseum in Ruins* by Maarten van Heemskerck. This Dutch artist spent four years in Rome, but painted this scene twenty years later. So perhaps some of the details, such as the huge statue of Jupiter and what looks like a bullfight, are purely imaginary. Above this painting, an eccentric work called *The Concert in the Egg* is thought to be based on a lost work by Hieronymus Bosch.

The next room contains several large Flemish altarpieces, many of them plundered from churches in Ghent and Antwerp after the French Revolution. The museum has put a couple of floppy modern chairs in the middle of the room, allowing us to collapse in front of Jan van Boeckhorst's *Martyrdom of St Maurice and his Companions*, a powerful work painted for the vanished church of Saint Maurice in Lille. We then move on to look at Gaspard de Crayer's *Miracle of the Fishes*, which was removed from a church in Ostend.

After another room with paintings in the style of Rubens, we reach a gallery with an *Annunciation* by the almost forgotten artist Pieter van Mole. We can recognise this work from the extraordinary lapis lazuli blue of the Virgin's cloak. This entire room is in fact devoted to lapis lazuli paintings, among them a *Christ surrounded by Angels* by Sébastien Bourdon which originally hung above the main altarpiece in the church of Saint André in Chartres.

We now enter a long gallery devoted to Chardin and his period. The main delight here is *The Silver Goblet*, a sober still life with a few simple objects. But it wasn't always such an austere composition; a recent x-ray examination has revealed that the artist originally included a large cabbage.

The next room is named after the Revolutionary painter Jacques-Louis David, but should perhaps be called the Watteau room, since it has several paintings by the two artists both confusingly known as 'Watteau of Lille'. François-Louis Watteau painted two works illustrating Alexander the Great's victories (over Darius and Porus), though we may well prefer the whimsical charm of his *Fête at the Colisée in Lille*, set in a country retreat to the west of the city that was briefly fashionable on the eve of the French Revolution, but had to be torn down in 1792 to prevent it being used by the Austrian army.

David's painting is a striking contrast, the first masterpiece of his austere neoclassicism. The subject

is Belisarius, the former general, blind and reduced to begging, at the moment when he is recognised by one of his soldiers. A far more frivolous neoclassical subject is Joseph-Marie Vien's *Psyche Recognising Love Asleep*. It is difficult to think that Vien was David's revered teacher. Diderot caught the newer mood when he wrote of Psyche: 'I don't see any evidence in her face of the mixture of fear, surprise, love and desire that one would expect.'

The next room is devoted to Lille paintings from the early eighteenth century. It includes Jean-Baptiste Wicar's enormous 1816 painting of *The Raising of the son of the widow of Naim*. Wicar was an artist from Lille who studied under David in Paris before moving to Italy. An even more fervent Revolutionary than his master, he served in the Italian campaign and advised on the requisitioning of Italian works of art. He took advantage of his contacts to acquire, perhaps not too scrupulously, a collection of more than one thousand drawings by Italian artists, including an impressive stack of Raphaels. His own paintings were mainly historical scenes, such as the one we see here, which originally hung in his Rome studio. It was admired by the Emperor of Austria and the Pope, but Wicar failed to find a buyer, and it was eventually bequeathed to the Lille museum in 1834, along with his collection of Italian renaissance drawings and a mysterious wax head we will see later.

The two little Goyas that hang at the end of the long gallery are the museum's greatest treasures. Well, one of them is. The other is sometimes more of an embarrassment. The painting on the right is called *The*

Young (or *The Letter*). It shows a servant holding a parasol to shade her mistress from the fierce Madrid sunshine as they walk past a group of women working at a public laundry. Its partner, shown opposite, is more difficult to admire. Known as *The Old* (or *Time*), it depicts an ancient Spanish woman with a horribly wrinkled face, dressed in her best clothes, looking at a miniature portrait of herself as a young woman. A servant behind her is holding up a mirror inscribed with the words: 'Que tal?' (What's happening?). Time himself seems about to sweep the two crones away.

The paintings look like a pair, but they were never intended as such. *The Old* was painted first (sometime between 1808 and 1812), whereas *The Young* is a later work (from 1813 to 1820). They were among a collection of paintings kept in Goya's studio, unseen by the public during his lifetime. When the artist's wife died, they were inherited by Goya's son Javier, who realised that *The Young* was a gem, but *The Old* would never find a buyer, so he cleverly decided to enlarge the latter and sell the two as a pair. Javier's additions are clearly visible, especially on the left side, but he appears to have fooled King Louis Philippe of France, who snapped up the two, and displayed them in an exhibition of his Spanish paintings held

119

in 1838. Young French artists were inspired by Goya's revolutionary technique and bold colours, but many visitors were shocked by the cruel realism of *The Old*, and it was finally withdrawn from the exhibition.

In 1872, when the two paintings were put on sale, the conservator of the fine art collection in Lille, Edouard Reynart, resolved to acquire them for his new (and as yet barely begun) museum. The city agreed to pay for *The Young*, but refused to spend public money on *The Old*. A private benefactor finally agreed to pay for the wrinkled old woman, and so provided Lille with one of the most astonishing paintings of the nineteenth century.

We may not even notice the little painting on the side wall titled *The Garotted Man*. It shows a crowd dispersing after a man has been strangled to death in public. The work used to be attributed to Goya, but for some reason is now considered a Velázquez.

The gallery behind us (as we look at the Goyas) contains a small collection of twentieth century paintings, including Picasso's *Portrait of Olga in a fur collar*, painted in 1923, five years after Picasso married his first wife. Picasso painted several affectionate portraits of Olga, a Russian dancer, but this one seems quite cold, almost like a classical statue, hinting perhaps that he was losing interest in her.

The Dutch room comes at the end of this gallery. It is quite surprising to find several impressive seventeenth-century works here, including a lovely skating scene by Jan van Goyen, a church interior by Emmanuel de Witte and a landscape by Jacob van Ruisdael. But the most striking work is Pieter Codde's little painting of *Melancholy*, showing a young Dutchman, probably the artist himself, sitting in a bare room, perhaps more bored than melancholic.

All that remains on this floor is the Impressionist collection. We have to go back to the Goyas to find this room, which contains several attractive works, including Monet's *Houses of Parliament in London*, which is one of eleven views of the Thames painted by the artist in 1904, and a curious painting on glass by Emile Bernard titled *The Pear Gatherers*. Finally, we come to a painting by Van Gogh that may well seem familiar. It was painted in 1890 when Van Gogh was staying with Dr Paul Gachet in Auvers-sur-Oise. Dr Gachet, who came from Lille, had at some time made a sketch of the *Five Studies of Cows* hanging in room 1. Van Gogh saw it in while he was staying at Auvers and made a painting from the sketch, probably in early July 1890, just a few weeks before he killed himself. Dr Gachet presented the work to the museum in 1951, allowing us to compare the two versions. The main difference is that Van Gogh added a black crow flitting ominously across the sky.

The museum owns a particularly rich collection of drawings, including no fewer than 1,300 works acquired in Italy by Jean-Baptiste Wicar and bequeathed to his home town. Most of these fragile works are kept in storage, but a few are occasionally displayed in temporary exhibitions held in a room next to the Impressionist collection. The Wicar bequest includes a collection of drawings by Raphael which was praised by Stendhal during a visit to Rome. There is also a portrait of Lucas van Leyden by Albrecht Dürer, a *Massacre of the Innocents* by Nicholas Poussin, and countless other delights only rarely seen by the public.

III. Medieval rooms. The next part of the visit takes us into the basement to look at the medieval rooms (though we might pause in the coffee shop on the ground floor). The first object we see in the basement is a beautifully lit fifteenth-century altarpiece from the Tirol illustrating the *Legend of St George*, who appears on horseback in the centre of the work. Then we come to a long vaulted room with a spectacular collection of medieval sculpture. On the right, just as we enter, a stone font from a church in the

Flemish village of Oplinter catches our eye. It has been placed on a thick tree trunk, which adds to its primitive grandeur. We have to crouch down, though, to look at the four carved faces filled with medieval sorrow.

Now we can wander through a collection of medieval Madonnas, each one standing on a block of wood cracked with age. A wooden Christ with both arms missing acquires a fresh impact from being hung against a dark green wall. And an aquamanile, originally used for serving water, looks particularly impressive with its shadow cast on the brick wall behind. But perhaps the most striking work in this room is a marble relief by Donatello hung against a suspended metal screen that looks like chain mail. Once in the collection of Lorenzo de' Medici, this work shows several scenes from the story of Herod's feast, when Salome presented the head of John the Baptist on a plate. We can see Renaissance ideas of perspective at work here, but also Donatello's curious technique of inscribing thin lines in marble.

We find two paintings by Dirk Bouts on the left wall. One illustrates *The Road to Paradise*, but we are perhaps more likely to be struck by *The Fall of the Damned*. Painted late in his life, it shows a man being swallowed alive by a fish, and several naked figures about to be dropped into a black pool. Finally, before we leave this room, we should look at the embroidery opposite, which once hung in front of an altar in a church near Lille. Probably designed by a pupil of Robert Campin of Tournai, it shows the Annunciation taking place against a background of blue silk damask.

There is one last work to look at on this level. It is a head of a young woman made of wax and was until recently it the room with the Chardins. However, the wax began to melt in the heat, and the head had to be moved to a room in the basement. This room was recently closed for restoration, and so we may have to approach one of the guards and beg for permission to look at it. The head depicts a shy enigmatic adolescent girl with sad downcast eyes. But who made it? It was presented to the museum in 1834 by Jean-Baptiste Wicar, who bought it while he was living in Rome painting huge canvases that no one wanted to buy. Wicar thought it was by Raphael, though there are other competing theories. One scholar ascribed it to Leonardo da Vinci; another claimed it was an ancient work modelled after the head of a Roman girl whose remains were found in 1485; a third suggested that it was a work by the seventeenth-century Flemish sculptor François

Duquesnoy, who lived in Rome. All these theories perhaps have to be rejected, if we accept the argument of a recent historian who claims that the drapery, which is carved of wood, could only have been done using tools invented in the eighteenth-century.

IV. The Salle des Plans-Reliefs. The final basement room contains a collection of twenty-six scale models of fortified towns resting on large wooden tables. Several centuries old, these remarkable relics constructed by anonymous craftsmen have survived wars, revolution, damp and decay. The first models, or 'relief plans', were made for Louis XIV after the Treaty of Aix-la-Chapelle in 1668 and showed the fortified towns in the Spanish Netherlands acquired by France under the terms of the treaty, including Lille, Tournai and Oudenaarde.

About fifty scale models were constructed during the reign of Louis XIV under the supervision of his secretary of war, the Marquis of Louvois. These exceptionally detailed works were built to a scale of 1:600 and showed tree-lined roads, brick farmhouses, city gates, and town halls, all in superb detail. The houses were made from wood covered with paper, while the trees and bushes were produced out of silk and cotton. Once the models were completed, they were transported in sections to the great gallery of the Louvre, but were treated as military secrets and so never shown to the public.

More models were made in the eighteenth century, when the craftsmen refined their techniques and harmonised their style, so that all the trees were made to look as they would in the month of May. The collection, which eventually grew to 127 towns, was transferred in 1776 to the Invalides, though twelve entire cities were lost in the move. Napoleon took a keen interest in the collection, appointing a conservator, a general director and thirteen specialists to maintain the models. He even commissioned a new model of the port of Cherbourg, larger than any of its predecessors.

Part of this extraordinary collection was almost lost following the final overthrow of the Emperor, when General Blücher, who had led the Prussians at Waterloo, took nineteen models back to Berlin as war booty, including a third version of Lille completed in 1743. The other models – then reduced to about one hundred – remained in the Invalides. They had lost all military significance by that time, but their cultural importance was eventually recognised, and in 1927 the entire collection was added to the list of protected monuments.

The nineteen models taken by Blücher were still in Berlin when Allied bombers attacked the city in 1944. The air raids destroyed eighteen of the model cities, sparing only the plan of Lille. It was returned to France after the war, though in a badly damaged state. So the model we see now has lost much of the surrounding countryside, parts of the fortifications and many of the large buildings. Yet it is still a fascinating relic that shows the city during the Ancien Régime.

When we stand in front of the model, where a bench has been placed, we can see the Porte de Roubaix directly in front, the fortifications where Euralille now stands to the left and the citadel in the distance. Most of the other models are so large that it is difficult to see the details that really interest us in the centres of the towns, but they give a fascinating impression of the extensive defence works that were needed for effective protection in the seventeenth century. The impressive model of Namur shows Vauban's complex system of defences spreading out from the hilltop citadel. Louis XIV captured this strategic fortress in 1692, leading to national jubilation and a long poem by Racine, but the citadel fell just three years later to the army of William of Orange. Vauban immediately summoned the minister of war to the Tuileries. 'There is a relief of Namur in the Tuileries,' he told the disgraced Minister. 'Would you have the courtesy to accompany me there. I will let you touch with your finger and see with your eye all the weaknesses of this place.'

V. Sculpture. All that remains is to look at two small collections on the ground floor. One is nineteenth-century sculpture. The other is ceramics. Both are reached through large rotundas at the back of the main hall. On the way to the sculpture room, on the right, we pass a plaster model of the Martyrs of Lille monument, but without the fifth figure lying on the ground. The model is crumbling and pitted with holes, which adds a certain sense of sorrow.

No such feelings are likely when we look at the knight on horseback in the rotunda. Made from plaster by the successful Parisian sculptor Emmanuel Frémiet, the knight looks ridiculous to the modern eye, though he appealed enormously to late nineteenth century taste. In April 1914, the Lille museum ordered a bronze version for its garden, but war broke out before the work could be done. By the time peace returned to Lille, the public had lost its enthusiasm for such dated images of chivalry.

Now we enter the sculpture hall, where the first

thing we see is a curious sculpture of a hermaphrodite, based on a classical original. Then we pass Joan of Arc and other historical French figures, until finally, in the far left corner, we find a lovely terracotta head by Camille Claudel. The subject is Louise, her nineteen-year-old sister, who had fashionably tousled short hair at the time.

The ceramics are on the other side of the main hall, but first, in the rotunda, we should stop to look at the bronze statue of Napoleon, posing as the protector of industry, with sugar beet and a spinning loom at his feet. Designed by Henri Lemaire in 1854, and apparently cast from cannons captured at the Battle of Austerlitz, the statue stood in the courtyard of the Vieille Bourse until 1986 (see page 21).

Now for lunch. We can eat a sandwich in the museum café, or something more substantial in the restaurant, which is in the new building on the other side of the courtyard, but it is perhaps more convivial to eat in one of the restaurants in the neighbourhood. We have already passed several places in the Rue de Béthune, such as the very lively Aux Moules, which is open from midday to midnight. There are several others, such as the excellent Passe Porc, opposite the Théâtre Sebastopol, a five minute walk from the museum.

The Belle Epoque
From the Théâtre Sebastopol to the Hospice Gantois

This is not a particularly arduous walk. We will look at one Art Nouveau house, stroll along some nineteenth-century streets, and perhaps visit one museum. All in all it is unlikely to take us much longer than two hours.

We begin where the last walk ended, standing outside the Théâtre Sebastopol. This grand theatre was built in 1903, apparently in a mere 103 days, after the old city theatre on Place du Théâtre burned down. It has a certain robust character, like the Victorian theatres of London, but not everyone appreciates the result. 'It is rather short on charm,' observes an information panel placed on the pavement outside. Perhaps so. But what about those muscular statues at the top of the steps, which the English text unexpectedly refers to as 'powerful ladies'. They may not be ladies, but they are quite impressive in their way.

We turn left, briefly following the straight Rue de Solférino, but then heading off right down the Rue des Postes. After a block, we turn left along the Rue des Pyramides, pausing to glance in the windows of an old piano shop, Pianos Schillio, which has kept its décor of old mirrors, floral wallpaper and a faded photograph of the splendid Lucien Schillio. A house on the opposite site, at No. 40, is signed by the architect Marcel Boudin, which may at first strike us as odd, since the house looks unassuming, but perhaps the curious brickwork at the top is the reason.

The houses in this street are less grand than those on the Rue de Solférino, but their painted shutters and neat appearance give them a pleasing French provincial charm. The odd house at No. 18 has a more Flemish character, dark and melancholy. It was built in 1892 by an architect who signed himself simply 'Newnham'. We have come a little too far, as we have to turn down the Rue Fabricy, which is just behind us. Our route takes us past a nineteenth-century school decorated with renaissance candelabra columns and strange dragon-like beasts, but we have come for something quite different, which we find by turning left into Rue Fleurus.

I. Maison Coillot. The Rue Fleurus is a dull street named after a forgotten French battle. It is lined with modest nineteenth-century neo-classical houses, but one house, No. 14, stands out. The Maison Coillot was completed in 1900 by Hector Guimard, the architect of the fanciful Art Nouveau métro entrances in Paris. Guimard began his career designing ordinary houses of the sort that would have fitted with this neighbourhood, but his style changed radically after a visit to Brussels in 1895. There he discovered the revolutionary architecture of Paul Hankar and Victor Horta. After making careful sketches, he returned to Paris and immediately launched the new style. After building several Art Nouveau houses in the capital, he was approached in 1898 by a Lille ceramics factory owner, to design a house that would serve as an advertisement for the firm Coillot. Guimard produced this eccentric house with curved stonework, an open terrace and a pointed roof, signing the work above the door. E. Gillet, who produced the fanciful ceramic decoration, added his name above the window. However, the style never caught on in Lille, and this house is the only genuine Art Nouveau building in the city. Sadly, it was lying empty the last time I passed, with only a few forlorn window boxes providing a hint of the previous occupants.

The Rue Fleurus leads into the Place Philippe le Bon, named after the duke who built the Rihour Palace, though the statue standing in the centre of the square is not the duke but Louis Pasteur. It was put up in 1922 close to the university where Pasteur made his first scientific discoveries. He had been appointed dean of the new faculty of science in 1854, and was approached by a Lille industrialist to look for a method of removing impurities that appeared during the fermentation of sugar. Pasteur discovered that the

fermentation was caused by microscopic organisms, and invented a process to kill off the bugs. He moved to Paris in 1857, where he carried out his research into what came to be called pasteurisation, but returned to Lille in 1894, by then a grand old man of science. The statue shows Pasteur standing on a high plinth, surrounding by statues of adoring women, one of them holding up a child. The reliefs on the base provide further reminders of Pasteur's achievements.

We cross to the other side of the square and continue down Rue Jean Bart, passing a vast and dilapidated medical faculty building of 1881, decorated with glazed bricks, gleaming mosaics and a clock that has stopped at 3.15. The former university library is further along this street on the left. Here we can make a short detour down Rue de Bruxelles, to the right, to look at the natural history museum, a wonderfully antiquated scientific collection located in a dusty nineteenth-century brick building. The vast collection includes some 2,000 rare birds, the skeleton of a whale and a collection of rare minerals neatly labelled in nineteenth-century ink.

Back on Rue Jean Bart, we continue to the end of the street, coming to a broad boulevard where we turn left. A very short detour down the Rue de la Liberté allows us to look at the impressive 1890 red brick mansion at No. 142. Signed Louis Cordonnier to the left of the entrance, it is decorated with a polished marble column, ornate ironwork and an elaborate set of iron bell-pulls (though these have been replaced by a modern intercom). But the strangest detail is the iron bracket attached to the marble column, which appears to end in a chicken's head.

A little further down, on the opposite side, the building at No. 219 was once a public bath-house. We can still see the Moorish-style tiles and the name Bains Lillois. It was designed in 1892 by Albert Baert, who many years later designed a spectacular Art Deco public swimming pool in Roubaix (described on page 164). Next door, a town house dated 1883 is decorated with ceramics painted with flowers.

We return to the end of the Rue de la Liberté and turn left to reach the Boulevard Papin. We are now approaching the Porte de Paris, an impressive city gate built by Simon Vollant in 1685-1692. Deliberately styled as a triumphal arch, it was intended by Louis XIV to provide a grand entrance to the most northerly city in his kingdom. The city wall on this side of town was demolished in 1858, leaving the gate standing isolated in the middle of landscaped flower beds. It has only recently been restored, bringing a shine back to the bronze trumpets at the top. It is worth crossing the road to look more closely at the two figures representing Mars and Hercules, and peer down into the sunken garden planted in the former ditch, though we shall have to cross back again.

After passing under a romantic oriel window on No. 2, we come to a stone monument in a little garden commemorating two former mayors – Gustave Delory and Roger Salengro – 'who made Lille a worthy capital of Flanders'. The monument was carved by

Robert Coin in 1959, though it looks thirty years older. Roger Salengro was a Socialist mayor in the early 1930's who launched an ambitious public works programme in Lille. Appointed interior minister in the socialist government of Léon Blum, he was fiercely attacked in right-wing newspapers and finally committed suicide in 1936.

We are just about to look at the town hall, but first we might make a little detour down the Rue du Réduit, to the right of the town hall. A little park contains a stone tablet salvaged from the old Porte de Tournai, one of Vauban's city gates. But there is something even more interesting further on, seen through a gap in the trees. It is a little baroque chapel that once belonged to the Fort du Réduit, a fortress built in 1707 on this site.

There is more to see in this neighbourhood. We continue straight ahead, but not too far, down the Rue des Déportés. This is one of the oldest quarters of Lille, though much was demolished in a slum-clearance plan, leaving just a few isolated old buildings. One of them is the ancient brick tower on the left, just beyond the school, which is all that survives of the medieval city wall. De Gaulle came here in 1959 to unveil a monument to the victims of the Resistance. (It is actually inside the tower, but the door appears to be permanently locked.) We now go back to the Rue Saint-Sauveur and turn right to find another unexpected building. The lovely baroque pavilion on the right is all that is left of the Hôpital Saint-Jean. The black and white tiled floor has survived, along with a carved relief showing two children.

II. Hôtel de Ville. We need no directions to find the town hall, which was built here in 1924-28, after the old town hall on the site of the Palais Rihour burned down. The architect modelled the building on traditional Flemish houses with step gables. The belfry, 102 metres high, was completed in 1932. At its base are two strangely elongated figures who represent Lyderic, on the left, with a falcon perched on his shoulder, and Phinaert, a ferocious giant with a thick moustache, on the right. According to an old legend, Phinaert ruled over this region in the seventh century, killing anyone who

passed through the wood of 'Sans Mercy'. He captured a woman called Emergaert, but she managed to hide her small child, Lyderic, who was raised by a deer. Lyderic finally killed the giant, rescued his mother, and founded the settlement of Lille.

It used to be possible to take a lift to the viewing platform near the top of the belfry, under the beacon light (seen in the photograph opposite shortly after the building was completed). Perhaps it still is. We can ask at the information desk inside the town hall (if we are here during office hours). While we are in the town hall, we might take a quick look at the giant figures of Lyderic and Phinaert in the main hall, which are paraded through the streets during local festivities.

We now go back to the Rue de Paris, passing the rosy façade of the Hospice Gantois on the left at No. 224. This old hospice was founded in 1460 by a benefactor from Ghent called Jean de la Cambe. Built to accommodate elderly women, it continued to serve this purpose until well into the twentieth century. It was not finally closed down until 1995, when it was restored as a luxury hotel. Unsurprisingly this offended some purists, though the conversion has been carried out with enormous sensitivity. there is not much to be seen from the street, apart from the

gothic gable end of the hospital wing of 1460, the

solid wooden door with its iron-grille window, and this strange wooden figure with a damaged nose on the door post. Most of the buildings date from the seventeenth century and are grouped around a series of quiet courtyards, one of which has been roofed over to create an atrium.

Now for another surprise further along the Rue de Paris. After crossing the Avenue John F. Kennedy, we come to an ancient baroque gate on the right, at No. 191, dated 1626. It leads into the courtyard of an eighteenth-century town house built as a refuge for Marchiennes Abbey. But the best is still to come. If we turn right down the Rue Gustave Delory, named after Lille's first working-class mayor, we come to an arched doorway at No. 58 dated 1673. This leads to a secret lane named the Rue des Brigittines after a convent that once stood near

here. We can walk to the end of the street, passing
neat seventeenth-century houses, but we must be
prepared for a shock as we turn the corner and find
a brutal tower block at the end of the lane. We now
return to the Rue de Paris and continue towards the
centre, past the familiar spire of the Eglise Saint-
Maurice.

Modern Lille

From the Gare de Lille-Flandres to the Espace Piranesienne

Before we leave Lille, we might just have time to look at the extraordinary new architecture on the edge of the old town. The Euralille complex, to use the unlovely official name, was planned in the early 1990's by the Dutch architect Rem Koolhaas. The main aim of the project was to build a high-speed train station on the site of a military barracks close to the centre of Lille. However, the master plan drawn up by Koolhaas also included office buildings, a shopping centre, two hotels and a new city park. Not everyone in Lille was enthusiastic about the result, but that is hardly surprising, as the aim of the project was to shock. 'It's meant to shake the city out of its habitual lethargy,' a spokesman explained. 'This city has no creative ambition. What is needed is a strong statement, based on a contemporary creativity.'

Rem Koolhaas was chosen to shake up Lille following an international competition in which he beat several major European architects, including Norman Foster. At the time he was selected, he was probably best known for his 1978 book *Delirious New York*, in which he praised the congestion and chaotic diversity of Manhattan. Suddenly, in his late forties, he found himself in charge of a massive government-backed project to bring the delirium of Manhattan to a depressed French city. And, in a way, he has succeeded. The Euralille complex has its faults, but it has definitely brought new energy to a city that seemed to be beyond hope. On this short walk, which takes about an hour, we will discover some of the finer details of the project.

I. The Porte de Roubaix. We begin, as always, on Grand'Place, perhaps stopping for a coffee in the café attached to the opera house. The broad Rue Faidherbe was created in 1880 to provide a grand Parisian-style boulevard linking the opera house with the old station. It is the most direct route, but it is possibly more interesting to follow the meandering trail along Rue Anatole France and Rue de Roubaix. Up until a few years ago, this would have led us into the red light district, but the quarter was cleaned up in 2003, and nothing of the old seediness has survived apart from a solitary neon sign flashing sadly above an abandoned sex shop.

Keeping to the left side of Rue de Roubaix, we might stop opposite the entrance to No. 26. A gap in the buildings on the right side allows us to glimpse a tiny clock tower with a bell. This belongs to an impressive town house whose history we can read on a plaque attached to the façade in the Rue du Lombard. It tells us that A. D. Scrive-Labbe, an industrialist from Lille, risked his life to smuggle out of England the first carding machine used in France. The plaque was put up in 1921, exactly one hundred years after the machine was installed in the building behind the high wall. A bronze relief shows the smuggler looking, well, slightly smug.

Opposite is a building where we would once have found out more about the Lille textile industry. The Musée Industriel et Commercial closed down some time ago, though someone is obviously still employed to trim the box hedges. Part of the collection ended up in the natural history museum we passed on walk 6. We now return to the Rue de Roubaix, passing an impressive old door at No. 39 and then, at No. 45, the imposing façade of the Hôtel d'Hailly d'Aigremont. This grand town house is now occupied by the military commander of the region, so it is unlikely that we will ever see inside. Dating from 1704, the mansion stands on land acquired by Henry Jacops, a rich merchant who bought himself the title of d'Hailly. His son added d'Aigremont to the family name and built the classical town house we see here around a cobbled courtyard, with a long garden at the back planted with trees. Little of this can be seen from the street, though we can get an impression of the

building from the Lille scale model in the Palais des Beaux-Arts, made some 40 years after the building was finished.

On the opposite side of the street, the Ecole Privé de Couture has a very traditional notion of fashion, judging from the finished clothes in the window. We cross the road ahead and reach a little square called the Place Saint Hubert, where the seventeenth-century house at No. 4 still has a handsome wooden door and the remains of an iron bell-pull. Just beyond, we come to the Porte de Roubaix, an old city gate of brick and stone that had in recent years become dilapidated, but was expertly restored for Lille's year as cultural capital of Europe.

We can walk through one of the three vaulted passages, or take a slightly longer route, though not, I would suggest, if we have young children with us. The long option involves climbing the sloping path to the left of the gate. This leads to the top of a stretch of ramparts which are, as several danger signs warn us, some ten metres above the moat, a fact which will not mean much to small children who want to run about. The land in front of the gate was once occupied by a complex network of moats, ditches and bastions, all built by Vauban to improve Lille's role as a fortress town. The cobbled road that

149

runs from the gate before coming to an abrupt end was once the main route to Roubaix. We can still see iron rails embedded in the cobblestones, a relic of the time when trams ran through the arches of the gate. The trams still run, but they now begin in a modern underground station at the far end of the park.

If we stand close to a fir tree, keeping well back from the ten-metre plunge, we can see much of modern Lille, including the spectacular curved roof of Lille-Europe station and the brightly-coloured façade of Euralille. We will say more about these buildings later, but we must first cross the little park, which is reached by a grand flight of stone steps at the far end of the ramparts. These lead us down to the Boulevard Carnot, where the French PTT built an elegant brick telephone exchange in the 1930's.

Now we walk through the Parc Henri Matisse, designed by the landscape architect Gilles Clément, who was responsible for the Parc André-Citroën in Paris. The most curious feature of the park is a forest of trees surrounded by a high concrete wall. Clément claims to have been inspired by a story he was told about a forest in Switzerland that was discovered in 1850 after a landslide. The trees had grown undisturbed for centuries, protected by a sheer face of rock. He decided to create a similar forest in Lille,

planting trees on a mound of earth surrounded by a
high wall. Known as the Ile Derborence, it is a slightly
absurd creation, as inaccessible as Vauban's citadel.
Koolhaas tried to distance himself from the project,
describing it as 'a typically French poetic idea, hyper-
egoistical, based on a series of metaphors.'

We now follow a gravel path that meanders through
the pine trees close to the ramparts. Soon we come
to a spot where we can look up at the front of the
Porte de Roubaix (below), now gleaming after the

151

recent renovation. This splendid brick gate was built, according to a small plaque on the front, in 1621, when Lille still belonged to the Spanish Netherlands. It was later restored, another plaque recalls, in 1875. The niche at the top is occupied by a fierce woman standing on top of a broken cannon with a sword in one hand and a spear in the other.

Keeping to the gravel path, we soon pass under a low bridge. We are now walking through the fortifications, as we can tell from a stretch of ruined wall on our right. We get a closer look at Jean Nouvel's Euralille building from here, with the hotel on the right, the business school on the left, and apartments above decorated with coloured panels reminiscent of a late Mondrian painting. The distinctive office block built on top of the station was designed for Crédit Lyonnais by Christian de Portzamparc. Built in the shape of the letter L, it is intended to symbolise Lille, though locals like to refer to it as the 'ski boot'. The windows of the 20-floor building are intriguing shapes, with hardly a right angle in sight, adding a certain childish whimsy that one would not expect of a bank.

The path now leads through a landscaped garden that is almost English in its rambling charm. But that stops as soon as we reach the Place Mitterand, a windswept square that people hurry across, ignoring the statue of the president who brought the high-speed train to Lille, and who appears to be slightly irritated as he strides in the direction of Euralille.

II. Gare Lille Europe. We now walk under the Le Corbusier Viaduct, a wobbly bridge perched on four graceful parabolic arches. An escalator leads up to the main station concourse, perched high above the platforms. Designed by Jean-Marie Duthilleul, chief architect of French railways, the station is an impressive futuristic steel and glass building. However, credit for the elevated glass concourse should probably go to Koolhaas, whose master plan required transparency, so that the constant flux of people and trains would be visible from the outside. It is an utterly modern vision, but for passengers waiting on a windy platform, it can be a bleak encounter with modernism. Not surprisingly, the most popular place to wait for the Eurostar is a fake Irish pub filled with relics of nineteenth-century country life.

Most people who use this station fail to discover its most striking feature. The Espace Piranesienne, designed by the architect Jean Pattou, forms a dramatic entrance to the metro station. A footbridge crosses a vast empty space with, below, various levels of escalators and bridges, some of them serving no obvious purpose. The walls are painted with large murals depicting an imaginary city that includes a few recognisable Lille buildings. Then we look down and see the buildings reflected in a dark pool, apparently disappearing into infinity.

It is a very disorienting space. The people going down the escalators seem small and forlorn, like figures descending into the inferno. We become more disoriented still on noticing, through a small glass window, cars speeding past on an urban motorway. Then we glimpse others walking along on a mysterious upper level that we cannot reach. Finally, just as we have controlled our vertigo, we hear the sudden terrifying din as a TGV passes through the station at three hundred kilometres an hour. This is what Koolhaas wanted. Everything is moving in different dimensions, at different speeds, leaving us totally confused.

We might continue up the escalator to look at the view from the back of the station, emerging on a small square with trees poking out of the wood decking. Looking to the right, we can see the ring road rising gracefully above a little park. It is an interesting spot, but not somewhere to hang around. It is a place for people in a hurry, carrying briefcases, talking into mobile phones, on their way somewhere else. It is not for people who like to wander, or sit on a bench, or feel the antiquity of a place.

Now we go back to the centre, perhaps pausing to admire the undulating station roof, once described by the SNCF, in a rare moment of corporate poetry, as a 'flying carpet'. The route back to the centre takes us back along the Le Corbusier Viaduct, which vibrates slightly, like the deck of a Channel ferry. There is no need to be genuinely alarmed. It is intentional, another structure designed to disturb us.

III. Gare de Lille-Flandres. We end up at the reassuringly neo-classical station (below), which was built

in 1867 just within the old city ramparts, replacing an older and much more modest station, hardly more than a single platform, built outside the walls. The army was initially reluctant to allow a breach in the city defences, but finally granted permission to the Northern Railway Company to build the new station. The company decided somewhat stingily to recycle the old Gare du Nord in Paris, which had became too small for the capital, rather than build a new station, but this was simply not good enough for the mayor of Lille. 'We are trying to create a great city here,' he told them.

A compromise was finally reached. The old station would be rebuilt, but with the addition of a ninth bay, a second floor and a monumental clock bearing the completion date of 1867. The station interior has remained virtually unchanged since then, though there are now high-speed trains running to Paris.

The opening of the Lille to Paris railway line in 1846 was an event of some importance in the northern town. The railway company even commissioned Hector Berlioz to compose a cantata. The composer – who looks very distinguished in the photograph opposite, taken by Nadar about thirteen years later – dropped everything to carry out the commission. 'I am very busy with *Faust*,' he wrote to a friend, 'but

I have just been forced to interrupt my work to write several feuilletons and a cantata which I am due to conduct in Lille for the celebration of the opening of the Chemin de fer du Nord.'

Berlioz spent three nights working on the *Le chant des chemins de fer* and conducted its première a week later, on 14 June, in the former ducal palace. 'I have been running around a little to keep my legs fit,' he wrote two weeks later to his sister. 'To begin with I have been for a week a resident of Lille, one of the busiest, and certainly the most serenaded – I have had to face four serenades, three of them instrumental and one vocal. The inhabitants of the great square on which  I was staying must have found my presence something of a liability.'

He was pleased with the performance of the cantata which was 'sung with uncommon verve and fresh voices which we are unable to find in Paris for our choruses.' He also conducted the final movement of

157

the *Symphonie funèbre et triumphale* with 250 musicians drawn from the army barracks. Then disaster struck. 'While I was in conversation in the room next door with the Dukes of Nemours and Montpensier, first my hat was stolen, then all the music of the cantata, the orchestral score, some of the parts for chorus and a full score. The upshot is that here is a lost work, as I don't feel the courage to start all over again. That is all I have gained from this dazzling festival which was sponsored by M. Rothschild, for which I was summoned from Paris and for which I have had to spend three nights composing the cantata.'

It was not quite as bleak as that. 'The Mayor of Lille has sent me in the name of the city a very fine gold medal with the inscription: Inauguration of the Northern Railway, the City of Lille to M. Berlioz,' he told his sister. The score was recovered a few years later, but the hat was never found. A version of the cantata was published in 1850 and the work was later incorporated in the song cycle *Feuillets d'Album*. A rare recording was made in 1966 by, appropriately, the French Railways Symphony Orchestra and the work was performed once again on platform one of Lille-Flandres station on 6 December 2003 to mark the beginning of the city's year as cultural capital of Europe. No other city would have dared such a thing.

Further Pleasures

The seven walks in this books are more than enough for one visit, but perhaps we will be tempted back a second time to explore the more remote corners of the city, beyond the city wall and the ramparts (which we see here in a calm 1930's photograph). We can reach most of these destinations by metro, followed by a short walk, although the museum in Villeneuve d'Ascq is easier by car.

I. Birthplace of General de Gaulle. Lille does not make much of the fact that General de Gaulle was born in 1890 in a house at 9 Rue Princesse, and most locals stubbornly refuse to accept that their beloved Grand'Place is now officially named Place du Général de Gaulle. Yet perhaps the new extension to the birthplace museum will help to raise the local profile of the former president. De Gaulle was born in a town house owned by his grandmother, opposite the St André church in a seventeenth-century quarter planned by Vauban. The rooms retain an austere Catholic atmosphere, bare apart from a few mementoes of De Gaulle's childhood, including the cot where the young Charles was lulled to sleep. The most exciting exhibit for most visitors is a bullet-riddled Citroën DS in which De Gaulle miraculously survived an assassination attempt, though cynics like to point out that most of the bodywork has been replaced. Crosses mark the spots where the bullets went through.

II. Wazemmes. There is more to this suburb than the Maison Folie by Lars Spuybroek (opposite, and see p. 180). The Place de la Nouvelle Aventure stands on the site of a vanished eighteenth-century country tavern that we may remember from a painting by François Watteau in the Hospice Comtesse. The north side of the square is now occupied by a nineteenth-century covered market (open every day except Monday), with shops selling French cheeses, dripping North Sea fish and freshly-plucked chickens, while the open space in front contains a flower market. The best time to be here is on a Sunday

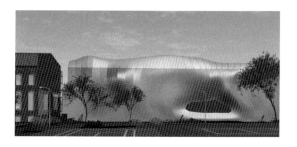

morning, when crowds emerge from the Gambetta metro station to hunt through the Wazemmes street market for bargains. There are stalls selling potatoes from the farms of Flanders, bargain lots of white socks, stacks of saucepans at rock-bottom prices and beautiful gilt mirrors which are, we are assured, genuine nineteenth-century items. Wandering through the crowded streets, we come as close as we ever will to the boisterous scenes of François Watteau, as stall-holders yell out bargains, a rosy-cheeked woman plays the accordion and someone cries out that their wallet has gone. *Take the metro to Gambetta and walk two minutes.*

III. Roubaix. Roubaix was once a prosperous textile-manufacturing town with a skyline bristling with tall chimney stacks. The industry dated back to the Middle Ages, when Charles the Bold granted John III of Roubaix the right to manufacture cloth. The city expanded rapidly during the industrial revolution, attracting many Flemish workers from over the border, and by 1914 the town had 250 factories. But the crisis of the 1960's hit the town hard, most of the factories closed down, and Roubaix became blighted by high unemployment and social unrest. The town responded in 2000, perhaps a little too boldly, by declaring itself a 'city of art and history'. It then went on to prove the point by turning a former Art Deco swimming pool into a beautiful museum, painting the houses on the Place de la Liberté in the brightest colours available, and converting several redundant brick factories into vibrant cultural centres.

The main reason to take the metro to Roubaix is to visit the Musée d'Art et d'Industrie. This astonishing museum opened in 2001 in a former Art Deco swimming pool built from 1927 to 1933 by Albert Baert. Instructed by the socialist mayor Jean Lebas to construct 'the most beautiful swimming pool in France', Baert based the plan on the dimensions of a Cistercian abbey, and decorated the interior in the fabulous style of a Moorish palace. The pool was closed for safety reasons in 1985 and lay forgotten for years before being renovated by Jean-Paul Philippon, an architect who had been involved in the conversion of the Musée d'Orsay. The inspired design includes nineteenth-century statues around the edge of the pool and changing rooms converted into display cabinets.

After passing through a dark entrance inspired by Cistercian architecture, we enter a vast hall with an Olympic pool illuminated by a huge sunburst window at the east end and a sunset window in the west. As we stand in front of the pool, which is still filled with water, we can hear the recorded cries of children leaping into the water.

The museum has an impressive collection of paintings, sculpture and ceramics, including some exceptional pottery by Picasso. Yet perhaps the most interesting feature is a collection of sample books containing some 50,000 samples of textiles from all over the world, the oldest dating back to Ancient Egypt. These books once belonged to the industrialists who ran Roubaix's mills. To complete the experience, we might decide to eat lunch in the elegant restaurant, La Piscine, run by the famous Meert shop. *Musée d'Art et d'Industrie, 23 Rue de l'Espérance, Roubaix. Closed Monday. Take the metro to*

Grand'Place. The journey from Lille Europe station takes 20 minutes.

IV. Villeneuve d'Ascq. The neat university town of Villeneuve d'Ascq was built in farmland outside Lille in the 1970's. It incorporates three villages, taking its name from one of them, Ascq, where 86 villagers were massacred by German soldiers on 1 April 1944. The university now has 50,000 students on a sprawling campus site, but there are still some remnants of rural life, including an interesting museum of windmills, which has three restored mills to visit, and a former red-brick farm that has been turned into a tourist office, museum of agriculture and 'Maison Folie'.

The splendid Lille metropolitan museum of contemporary art is located in a low brick building set in rolling parkland. The bulk of the collection comes from two bequests by early twentieth-century collectors, Roger Dutilleul and his nephew Jean Masurel, who filled their Parisian apartments with superb Cubist works by Picasso, Braque and Léger. The museum has added other works from the period, including rare sculptures by Laurens and Lipschitz. It has seven works by Modigliani, including his *Nu assis à la chemise*; and it has a strong collection (about to be expanded) of art brut. Once we have looked around the museum, we may be tempted by an attractive café which looks out on the park. *1 Rue du Musée, Villeneuve d'Ascq. Open Wednesday to Monday 10-6. A short metro ride to Pont de Bois station, then a six-minute ride on bus 41 to the park gates.*

V. Lille for children. A visit to Lille with children can be immensely enjoyable if you take them to the right places. They will probably not want to look at paintings in the Palais des Beaux-Arts, but might be tempted by the prospect of a room full of seventeenth-century scale models of cities captured by Louis XIV. And while they may object to long walks in the old town, they may be persuaded to take a trip on the fully-automated metro, especially if you let them stand at the very front of the train, where the driver normally sits. Perhaps the large mural of imaginary cities at Lille-Europe station will interest some children. If not, they may be diverted by the sight of a TGV passing through the station at 300 kilometres an hour.

Lille does not have too many parks, but the Bois de Boulogne is an adventurous woodland on the edge of the old citadel. There is a miniature train, a playground for older children, a small fairground and a zoo. A walk through the outer defences of the Citadel may prove a success with small boys, especially if you take the time to explain the system of moats and bastions. Parents should also squeeze in a visit to the Natural History Museum, which is pleasingly chaotic, like a cabinet of curiosities.

Then there is the matter of food. Children can go anywhere in France, but some places are especially friendly. The Crêperie Beaurepaire is a good place for a simple Breton pancake, served with almost any type of filling a child might request.

VII. The Lille Braderie. In a tradition that dates back to the Middle Ages, the streets of Lille are turned into an enormous flea market for a few days in early September. The Braderie had its origins in an old annual custom in which rich people allowed their servants to clear out the attics of junk and sell it on the street. A charming painting by François Watteau in the Hospice Comtesse shows that the Braderie had by the eighteenth century evolved into a colourful street festival. It is now the largest flea market in Europe, if not the world, with about one million people milling around streets overflowing with junk. You'll see dusty beer bottles, old hats, a record player that broke in the early 1970's, crucifixes that once hung in a grandmother's bedroom, used shell cases from World War One, coat hooks, necklaces made from shells gathered on Wimereux beach in 1962, mysterious metal objects salvaged from textile factories, almost all of it once precious to someone. *Held on the first weekend of September. Most of central Lille is car-free for the weekend.*

Lille 2004

Lille 2004 is one of the most ambitious programmes ever drafted for a European capital of culture. It involves a dense diary of classical music, exhibitions, street art, drama, dance, film and festivals. But the city has also invested heavily in urban renewal, restoring some seventy historic monuments – including the opera house and all the city's old churches. The Rue Faidherbe has been turned into a handsome urban promenade, the Quai de Wault waterfront is now a romantic place to linger, and seven redundant buildings have been converted into dynamic cultural centres. The result is an astonishing revitalisation of a city that was not so long ago in deep recession.

It's impossible to list everything planned for 2004, but it might be useful to highlight some of the events that are likely to startle, provoke, amuse or confuse.

They include a procession of giants arriving by boat, an international soup festival, a mobile restaurant that tours the city looking for a place to park, a Chinese street, a modern pigeon loft and a literary evening inspired by the Duke of Burgundy's famous Feast of the Pheasant. The venues are equally diverse, taking in city streets, shop windows, abandoned factories and a metro station. Nor does the programme stop at the boundaries of the Lille metropolitan area. There are events taking place in 150 towns in northern France, some as far off as Calais and Arras, and a few located across the border in the Belgian cities of Kortrijk, Tournai and Mons.

We should begin with a stop at the 2004 information office close to Lille Europe station, where we can stuff our pockets full of leaflets and perhaps buy a pass. We might then take a quick look inside the exhibition centre Le 2004 in Euralille where many of the events are happening. If we are here during the weekend, we should find out what theme is scheduled for Les Mondes Parallèles, a weekend festival that runs from dusk on Friday to dawn on Monday. The themes are enormously diverse, so we might find ourselves stumbling on a Japanese weekend (29-30 May), a Tango championship (11-13 June), a parade of giants (13-14 July), a Marrakesh weekend (20-22 August), or even an accordion festival (21-23 May). Remember that the Lille Braderie takes place on the first weekend of September. The city is packed in a normal year, and might just be impossible in 2004.

Street art

I. Tour Lille Europe. The first evidence of Lille 2004 comes as the train pulls into Lille Europe station. A 20-floor office tower designed by Claude Vasconi has been transformed by Kurt Hentschläger. He has installed 1,800 neon lights to create a beacon that he hopes will be as impressive as the ancient lighthouse at Alexandria. *Euralille, until November.*

II. Metamorphosis of Lille Flandres station. The transformation of Lille continues at the old Lille Flandres station, where the light designer Hervé Descottes has installed panels in the glass roof to bathe the station in a mellow purple light. The aim perhaps is to show people arriving from Paris by TGV that Lille is not the grey city they may have been anticipating. *Lille Flandres station, until November.*

III. Source de l'Abondance. The Lille-born comic strip artist François Boucq has designed a witty fountain for the square in front of the old Lille Flandres station. Yet more evidence that Lille is a city of wit and colour. *Lille Flandres station, June to November.*

IV. The streets of Shanghai. When we walk down the Rue Faidherbe (the broad boulevard running from Lille Flandres station to Grand'Place) we may well find that it has been transformed into a gaudy Chinese street. The city of Shanghai aims to recreate Nankin Street by installing neon signs, street lamps and Chinese shops. *Rue Faidherbe, from March to May, then moving to Dunkirk citadel in June.*

V. Dead chickens. An eccentric artists' collective from Berlin Mitte has come up with a plan to install a menagerie of five mechanical chickens on Rue Faidherbe. Created out of latex and metal, and animated by electric motors and hydraulic pistons, these bizarre creatures are likely to draw large crowds. *Rue Faidherbe, July and August.*

VI. The suspended forest. If we visit Lille in the summer, we will find that the Grand'Place and the Place du Théâtre are covered with an eccentric forest of suspended trees, hung upside down by their roots and lit by spotlights. Created by two graphic designers from Angers who sign themselves 'Lucie Lom', this forest filled with twittering birdsong is likely to be one of the memorable sights of 2004. *Grand'Place, Lille, in May and June, then Place Hentgès in Hellemmes from mid-July to mid-September.*

VII. Luminous circle. The French conceptual artist Daniel Buren has created a circle of light on a patch of wasteland next to the Musée Hospice Comtesse. This is one of several artworks commissioned for historic locations in the old town. *Ilôt Comtesse, until November.*

VIII. The mobile diner. The French artist François Azambourg has constructed a miniature restaurant on wheels which he plans to park in different locations in the city. The diners sit in glass-walled rooms on two levels, eating with edible cutlery. *Random locations in Lille, until November.*

IX. Waiting for the metro. Two artists, Louis-Philippe Demers and Robert Lepage, have created a strange colony of robots waiting for a train on a disused metro station platform. *Fives metro stations, until November. Only accessible with a valid public transport ticket.*

X. Place des Bleuets. A strange neon construction

by François Morellet lights up a square in Vieux Lille. The circles of light are calculated according to the decimal numbers of Pi. *Place des Bleuets, until November.*

XI. Porte de Roubaix. A Japanese artist, Keiichi Tahara, has created a light installation for the Porte de Roubaix, a sixteenth-century city gate close to Euralille. The installation is intended to emphasise the transition from the city to the park, and from reality to dream. *Porte de Roubaix, until November.*

XII. La Cage Nature. The artist Vincent Dupont-Rougier has created strange metallic structures with shrubs growing at the top. He has attached a ladder so that couples can disappear into the bushes. *Various locations in Lille, until November.*

Exhibitions

I. Rubens. The Palais des Beaux-Arts is marking the year with the most complete exhibition on Rubens since 1977. Its own sizeable collection will be supplemented with dozens of other paintings, sketches and tapestries. The aim of the exhibition is to highlight Rubens' diversity as an artist, writer, diplomat, inventor and colourist. Long queues are likely. *Palais des*

Beaux-Arts, until 14 June. Closed Tuesdays.

II. Christian de Portzamparc. A major exhibition on the French architect who designed the Crédit Lyonnais tower ('the ski boot') at Euralille, the Cité de la Musique in Paris and the LVMH tower in New York. His tower blocks may be controversial but they are never boring. *Palais des Beaux-Arts, 8 September to 5 January 2005.*

Events

I. Giants. A village is being created outside Lille to accommodate an international gathering of ceremonial giants from northern Europe, Spain and even China. The giant figures are expected to arrive on a flotilla of boats down the River Deûle. *Lille, 10-11 July.*

II. Collages de France. An unusual film project called Collages de France has been organised for Lille 2004 by Le Fresnoy arts centre in Tourcoing. It involves ten films on the theme of contemporary France made by the French film-maker Jean-Luc Godard in his home in Switzerland. A fast internet connection is to be created, allowing the public to interact with the director while he is working on the films. Godard aims to complete one film every month, with the première in the Pompidou Centre in Paris, followed by a screening the next day in Le Fresnoy centre. *Le Fresnoy, 22 Rue de Fresnoy, Tourcoing. Alsace metro station.*

III. Tango weekend. A tango festival in Lille may seem a little unexpected, but this is a town where couples gather every Sunday to tango in the courtyard of the Vieille Bourse. The Tango Weekend takes place in various venues, including the Hospice d'Havré in Tourcoing, a former convent that will be turned into a tango cabaret. *Venues in Lille, 11-13 June.*

IV. Lovers. A mysterious installation by the Japanese collective Dump Type involves naked figures inside a cube who are seen walking, running and occasionally embracing. *Le 2004, Euralille, to 8 August.*

V. Le Labyrinthe Olfactif. Serge Lutens, a designer and perfume-maker born in Lille, is constructing a curious concrete labyrinth sprayed with various smells from his childhood. The aim is to evoke the nostalgic smell of rain, earth, leaves and fairgrounds. *Le 2004, Euralille, until November. Closed Monday and Tuesday and possibly in August.*

178

Out of Lille

I. Antoine Watteau. A large exhibition on Antoine Watteau's scenes of courtly life is to be held in the fine arts museum of the town in which he was born. The exhibition aims to shaw that Watteau invented a new genre which enjoyed enormous success in eighteenth-century France. *Museé des Beaux-Arts in Valenciennes, until 14 June. Closed Tuesday.*

II. Ingres. The fine arts museum in Cambrai owns a famous painting by Jean-Auguste Ingres of the *Head of the Grande Odalisque.* It is one of nine different versions on the same theme, the most famous being *La Grande Odalisque* of 1814 in the Louvre. All nine versions have been brought together in an exhibition that reveals Ingres' extraordinary use of colour. *Musée des Beaux-Arts in Cambrai, 26 June to 31 October. Closed Monday and Tuesday.*

III. Matisse. An exhibition in the recently reno-vated Musée Matisse in Cateau Cambrésis aims to establish a link between Matisse's vivid canvases and the bright dyes used in the local textile industry. Matisse was born in Cateau Cambrésis, where the textile factories specialised in high quality fabrics destined for Paris. The exhibition features some 50 paintings, drawing and engravings, along with Matisse's own collection of fabrics, shown here for the first time. *Musée Matisse, Cateau Cambrésis, 23 October 2004 to 23 January 2005. Closed Tuesday.*

Maisons Folies

The 'Maisons Folies' project is perhaps the most inspiring idea to come out of Lille 2004. The organisation has restored twelve former factories and listed monuments to create a network of permanent community centres. Named after the aristocratic follies of the eighteenth-century, the centres will have art galleries, workshops, libraries, theatres and cafés. Some of the most exciting events of Lille 2004 are likely to be staged in these extraordinary spaces, seven of which lie within the Lille metropolitan area, while the others are further off, in Arras, Maubeuge and three cities in Belgium (Mons, Tournai and Kortrijk). No matter what is going on, the Maisons Folies are worth visiting simply to admire the architecture, drink a coffee and soak up the atmosphere.

I. Wazemmes. A Rotterdam architect, Lars Spuy-broek, was brought in to transform the nineteenth-century Leclercq textile factory in the suburb of Wazemmes, abandoned since 1990. He came up with an inspiring plan involving an undulating wire mesh screen on the façade, a new street and a square. It was still a mouldering ruin when I was shown around, with pigeons fluttering through the industrial spaces, but Lars Spuybroek was quietly confidence that it would be transformed into somewhere magical. *Maison Folie de Wazemmes, Rue de l'Hôpital St Roch, Wazemmes. Metro to Wazemmes and a five-minute walk.*

II. Brasserie des Trois Moulins. A former eighteenth-century brewery in the suburb of Moulins has been turned into an exciting centre with recording studios, space for clubbing, inner courtyards for performances and a modern bar and brasserie. *Brasserie des Trois Moulins, Rue d'Arras, Lille-Moulins.*

III. La Condition Publique. Another Maison Folie will occupy a massive industrial building of 1902 in Roubaix where wool and silk were once packed. The building has an impressive internal cobbled street covered with a glass and iron roof, though the most eccentric feature is its sloping roofs covered with turf. The architects aim to create a hanging garden inside the building, along with exhibition halls and

181

a traditional northern French estaminet. The author Michel Quint is writing a thriller in twelve parts situated in the building. The episodes will be published at www.laconditionpublique.com. *Place Faidherbe, Roubaix. Take the metro to Roubaix Eurotélé-port then bus 29 to Faidherbe.*

IV. L'Hospice d'Harvé. A remarkable seventeenth-century convent in the suburb of Tourcoing has been concerted into a Maison Folie. Events will take place in the chapel, hospice and hidden gardens. *Rue d'Harvé, Tourcoing. A short walk from the Tourcoing Centre metro stop.*

V. Le Colysée. A modern Maison Folie in a green location on the banks of the River Deûle. It takes its name from a country tavern that was briefly fashionable in the late eighteenth century. *Lambersart.*

VI. Le Fort de Mons. A vast nineteenth-century military fortress has been converted into a cultural complex with a music school, exhibition area and restaurant. *Rue de Normandie, Mons-en-Baroeul. A short walk from the Fort de Mons metro stop.*

VII. La Ferme d'en Haut. An eighteenth-century

farm built around a vast inner courtyard has been converted into a Maison Folie serving the new university town of Villeneuve d'Ascq. The complex also contains the local tourist office and a museum of agriculture. Exhibitions, theatre, workshops and demonstrations of local cooking are planned for 2004. *268 Rue Jules Guesde, Villeneuve d'Ascq.*

Information office

The Lille 2004 information office, in a post office sorting building next to Euralille, sells several types of passes for visiting events. The Lille 2004 free access pass – valid for one, two or three days – gives entry to all 2004 venues and free travel on public transport. It costs 22 for one day, and you will have to provide a passport photo. For 6 the Lille 2004 day pass offers reduced entry prices to some venues and free travel on public transport. The centre also sells a quirky assortment of Lille 2004 souvenirs designed by European artists and manufactured locally.
Tri Postal, Avenue Willy Brandt, tel 08 90 39 20 04 (from France), 00 33 359 579400 (from abroad), www.lille2004.com.

Staying in Lille

The most romantic hotels in Lille are located on the quiet lanes and cobbled squares of Vieux Lille. These hotels tend to get booked up long in advance, especially at weekends, so planning ahead is essential. Prices are similar to those in other northern European cities such as Brussels and Ghent. Some hotels reduce their rates at weekends, and it is worth checking out for deals though specialised travel agencies such as Directline Citybreaks (directline-holidays.co.uk) or Euro Destination (eurodestination.com). Most room rates exclude the price of breakfast, so we can, if we prefer, eat out in a café such as Paul or Le Pain Quotidien. The phone numbers given here are for making calls within Lille. When calling from abroad, add the international code for France (00 33) and drop the first 0 of the local number.

Alliance, 17 quai du Wault. Tel. 03 20 30 62 62. A former seventeenth-century Franciscan convent in an attractive quayside location has been skilfully converted into a modern hotel. The cloister has been covered with a glass roof to make a striking restaurant. Nonetheless, it is perhaps too much of a business hotel to appeal to weekenders, though some may appreciate the availability of a trouser press in the bedroom. A ten-minute walk from the centre. 80 rooms. Double room at least €150.

Bellevue, 5 Rue Jean Roisin. Tel. 03 20 57 45 64 or www.grandhotelbellevue.com. A grand old hotel on the south side of Grand'Place. It stands on the site of the Hôtel de Bourbon, where Mozart, then aged nine, stayed in August 1765. The Bellevue is now owned by an international chain, but has kept something of the charm of an old French hotel. Those in search of period details should enjoy the creaking iron-cage lift, the collection of old photographs of hotel rooms, and the faded Air France calendar by the desk. Room are comfortable, though many look out on a dark courtyard. It's perhaps worth paying a few euro extra for one of the 15 rooms with a view of Grand'Place. A double with a view costs at least €116.

Le Brueghel, 5 Parvis Saint-Maurice. Tel. 03 20 06 06 69 or www.hotel-brueghel.com. An attractive Old Flemish style building dating from the 1920's, though it looks much older. The interior is imaginatively decorated with a somewhat eccentric collection of antiques. Conveniently close to the stations and Grand'Place, it's a favourite address for actors, musicians and anyone looking for somewhere a bit unusual. A double costs €66.50.

Carlton, 3 Rue de Paris. Tel. 03 20 13 33 13. This grand neo-baroque hotel with its striking copper dome is located bang in the centre, facing the opera house. It was built in the 1920's, but the interior harks back to the eighteenth century. It is, not surprisingly, a favourite hotel for opera singers who come to perform in Lille. The round room below the dome is outrageously luxurious and utterly unaffordable. 57 rooms. Double room at least €186.

L'Hermitage Gantois, 224 Rue de Paris. Tel 03 20 85 30 30. A former hospice for old people was transformed in 2003 into a striking modern hotel. Located near the Porte de Paris, the hotel has a conference room located in the fifteenth-century hospital ward, a glass-roofed lounge in a former courtyard, and a banquet room in the former refectory. The rooms have wooden beams and are attractively decorated with old paintings and tapestries. Some have windows that open onto leafy courtyards. 67 rooms. Double room €190.

Hôtel de la Treille, 7-9 Place Louise-de-Bettignies. Tel. 03 20 55 45 46. This friendly hotel opened in 1988 in a modern building in the heart of Vieux Lille. It's the perfect location for discovering the secret squares of the old town or eating out in the convivial restaurants of Rue de Gand. The only problem with this hotel is that the bedrooms are really quite small. They are furnished in a plain modern style. Double room €76.

Ibis Opéra, 21 Rue Lepelletier. Tel. 03 20 06 21 95. A modern hotel just off Grand'Place in one of the city's most attractive streets. Run by a French chain that owns several other hotels in the city, but this is the best for location. The rooms are modern and utterly bland. Children under 12 can stay in the parents' room free. Double room €75 in the week, dropping to €56 at weekends.

Lille Europe, Avenue Le Corbusier. Tel. 03 28 36

76 76. A modern functional hotel located in the Euralille complex, just a few minutes from the stations. The breakfast room has large glass windows looking out on the Parc Matisse. Double room from €69.

Hôtel de la Paix, 46 Rue de Paris. Tel. 03 20 54 63 93. A seductive small hotel near the St Maurice church in a building that dates from 1782. The rooms were recently redecorated in a traditional French style. A very good hotel for people who want to be in the heart of the city. Double room from €68.

Le Royal, 2 Boulevard Carnot. Tel. 03 20 14 71 47. A grand hotel located on a quiet street just behind the opera house. It is now part of the Mercure group, but still retains its original fin-de-siècle grandeur, with thick carpets, heavy curtains and a magnificent stained glass window on the staircase. The bedrooms are comfortable, but slightly old-fashioned. Most rooms have large Art Nouveau windows and balconies looking onto the street. The twin-bed rooms are more spacious though perhaps less romantic than ones with a double bed. 101 rooms. Double room from €129, dropping to €113 at weekends.

LILLE — Grand'Place - Marchand de Frites

Eating out in Lille

Some of the most seductive restaurants in France
are located in the streets of Lille. We probably won't
have time to discover them all, but we should at least
aim to have breakfast in a branch of Paul, try a
Breton pancake in the Crêperie Beaurepaire, dine out
in a typical Lille restaurant such as La Cave aux
Fioles, and perhaps, if we can possibly fit it in, order
a pot of mussels at Aux Moules. After all of that, we
may feel unable to eat one more petit pois, though it
would be a pity to leave Lille without trying at least
one of the famously tasty gaufres sold at Meert.

The cooking in Lille tends to reflect the history of
the city. There is a solid local tradition that is close
to Flanders and Brussels, and a more sophisticated
style that comes from Paris and other regions of
France. Tourists from Belgium feel very much at

home as soon as they see that the menu lists dishes such as moules-frites (mussels and chips) and carbonnade à la flamande (beef stewed in dark Flemish beer), though they may smile when they see the spelling of waterzoi (a stew of fish or chicken, but spelt waterzooi in Flanders).

This region of northern France also has some specialities of its own, such as flammekueche (a traditional Flemish peasant dish dating from the eighteenth century perhaps related to the pancakes that appear in Bruegel paintings), potjevleesch (a selection of three types of white meat in aspic) and some distinctive local cheeses such as Maroilles.

The beer culture in Lille is likewise heavily influenced by Belgium. We will find excellent cafés serving a range of different beers, including a few that are brewed in the countryside outside Lille. No serious beer drinker should leave Lille without a visit to Les Trois Brasseurs, a small brewery opposite the old Lille Flandre station, where we can sit under a shiny copper vat and ask for a palette. The waiter will return carrying a small wooden tray with four small glasses of the brewery's beer, allowing you to savour the difference between *blonde, brune, ambrée* and *blanche.*

We will find clusters of restaurants and bars in several areas of the city, such as the Rue de Gand,

around the Théâtre Sebastopol and the Rue de
Béthune. We should follow the example of the locals
and book a table in advance, especially in the evening.
It is also worth remembering that many restaurants
are closed on Sunday.

I. Grand'Place neighbourhood

L'Alcide, 5 Rue des Débris Saint Etienne. Tel. 03 20
12 06 95. A certain Monsieur Alcide opened this
restaurant in 1880. It became a Lille institution, with
its neon advertisement shining above an arcade on
Grand'Place. The interior has long rows of tables,
mirrors and benches along the walls. Everything, in
fact, that we look for in a traditional French restaurant.

Brasserie André, 71 Rue de Béthune. Tel 03 20 54
75 51. A handsome restaurant dating from the 1930's
with a wood-panelled interior, mirrors and white
tablecloths. The well-to-do regulars come here for
classic French cooking.

La Chicorée, 15 Place Rihour. Tel 03 20 54 81 52.
The lights stay on in this busy brasserie close to
Grand'Place long after most people have gone to

bed. We can eat moules-frites or a steak at any time of the day or night. The waiters continue to serve up until 4 am on weekdays, and even later on Friday and Saturday. Prices go up after midnight.

Les Compagnons de la Grappe, 22 Rue Lepelletier. Tel 03 20 21 02 79. A tempting little wine bar in a quiet courtyard close to Grand'Place. You can eat typical French bistro cooking in the wood-panelled rooms, or settle down in the courtyard for a summer evening glass of wine.

La Compostelle, 4 Rue Saint-Etienne. Tel. 03 28 38 08 30. An attractive restaurant in a sixteenth-century inn that once accommodated pilgrims travelling to Santiago de Compostela. The striking Renaissance façade, open courtyard and warren of different coloured dining rooms make this one of the most seductive restaurants in Vieux Lille. The setting is perhaps more appealing than the cooking, though there is nothing wrong with the sole meunière.

Crêperie Beaurepaire, Rue Saint-Etienne. Perfect for a quick lunch, this attractive restaurant has wood beams, bare brick and bold red walls. The menu lists about forty different types of buckwheat galettes, served with cheese or bacon or exotic fillings. You can have an inexpensive lunch here by ordering a simple galette and a small bowl of cider. The terrace occupies a sunny eighteenth-century courtyard. A second branch called Crêperie de Beaurepaire II, at 6 Place Lion d'Or, is equally enticing, and equally popular. You will need to arrive soon after opening time to get a table without booking.

Aux Moules, 34 Rue de Béthune. Tel. 03 20 57 12 46. This convivial northern brasserie preserves the atmosphere of pre-war Lille. With its white tiled walls, polished brass rails and old photographs of the city streets, it has not changed much since it opened in 1930 in the reconstructed Rue de Béthune. The cooking is close to Belgian style, with specialities like rabbit stewed in Flemish beer, kidneys cooked in Gueuze and mussels served in heavy black cooking pots. Astonishing quantities of mussels are cooked during the Lille Braderie, and the empty shells are dumped in an enormous pile in the street.

II. Vieux Lille

A l'Huîtrière, 3 rue Chats Bossus. Tel. 03 20 55 43 41. A secluded restaurant at the back of an Art Déco

195

fishmonger's shop, L'Huîtière is somewhere for a very special occasion. It has been around for decades, but continues to produce the sort of refined cuisine that merits a star in the red Michelin guide. The menu tempts us inside with specialities like oysters and bouillabaisse. It is, inevitably, an expensive indulgence.

Le Lion Bossu, 1 Rue Saint-Jacques. Tel. 03 20 06 06 88. A tempting restaurant occupying the first floor of a seventeenth-century brick house in the heart of Vieux Lille. The cooking is inventive French style.

La Cave aux Fioles, 39 Rue de Gand. Tel. 03 20 55 18 43. Closed Saturday lunch and Sunday. One of the most seductive restaurants in Lille. We enter down a narrow corridor lined with posters advertising Lille exhibitions. This leads into a cobbled courtyard, now roofed over, that separates two houses, one from the seventeenth century and the other built about a century later. The restaurant occupies an intimate front room with exposed brick walls, lit by dim red lamps. The owner's choice of jazz adds something to the romantic allure. When this restaurant opened in 1981, the Rue de Gand was not the fashionable restaurant quarter it is now. It seems a miracle that it has survived so long when it offers a lunch menu for a mere ten euro. The owner even offers to pick up diners from their hotel in, of all things, a London taxi. This is a place to book now, before you forget.

Estaminet du Rijsel, 25 Rue de Gand. Tel 03 20 15 01 59. This looks like an ancient Flemish country tavern, but it was actually created a few years ago. The rooms have all the trappings of a Flemish inn, or estaminet, including a large iron stove and a miscellaneous collection of farming equipment. The menu features old favourites like chicory soup, carbonnade à la flamande and hochepot, all prepared using produce from northern French fields.

La Pâté Brisée, 63-65 Rue de la Monnaie. Tel 03 20 74 29 00. An attractive restaurant with a lime green front and rooms decorated in traditional Flemish style. A good spot to stop for a light lunch of quiche or salad.

La Terrasse des Remparts, Porte de Gand, Rue de Gand. Tel. 03 20 06 74 74. A striking restaurant located in an old city gate, reached by an ancient flight of stone steps. Praised by locals for its sensitive restoration, attentive staff and seductive terrace. The menu changes according to the season, offering an interesting range of northern French specialities. Open until late.

La Table du Siam, 79 Rue de la Monnaie. Tel 03 20 55 75 57. A cosy wood-panelled Thai restaurant in the heart of Vieux Lille. Booking essential at weekends.

III. Palais des Beaux-Arts neighbourhood

Le Passe Porc, 155 Rue Solférino. Tel. 03 20 42 83 93. It is difficult to walk past this intimate bistro without being tempted inside. Facing the Sébastopol theatre, it has a deeply alluring interior, with mirrors, benches covered with red velvet and a collection of pig ornaments. The only possible problem is that it features the sort of authentic northern French cooking that makes some people shudder, including andouillettes, tripes artisanales, and pochjt-vlees maison. A five-minute walk from the fine art museum.

IV. Citadel neighbourhood

Au Quai du Wault, 20 Quai du Wault. Tel. 03 20

30 16 11. This appealing Flemish restaurant looks at least a century old, but it only opened a few years ago on the restored Wault quayside. It offers very simple Flemish-style cooking, proposing, for example, a lunch of soup and bread.

V. Stations neighbourhood

Les Trois Brasseurs, 22 Place de la Gare. Tel. 03 20 06 46 25. A large and convivial tavern opposite the Lille Flandres station, with dark wood, solid tables and a collection of souvenirs of the Paris to Roubaix cycle race. The tavern brews three varieties of beer on the premises. The Blonde is a typical pale yellow Flanders beer, Ambrée is a darker beer, and their Scotch a potent ale. The tavern serves enormous portions of French brasserie food, including a jarret grillé avec pommes sautées et choucroûte that leaves most people feeling stuffed. The tavern is a good place to eat with children and a pleasant spot to sit with a beer before catching the Eurostar home.

Cafés

Méo, 5 Grand'Place. Open Monday 1-6.45, Tuesday to Saturday 8.30-6.45. A small coffee bar in the corner of a delicatessen serving a range of specialised coffees. Run by a Lille firm that has been roasting coffee since 1928.

Pâtisserie Meert, 27 Rue Esquermoise. Open Tuesday to Sunday. An elegant nineteenth-century tea room that has barely changed since it opened in 1909.

Paul, 8 Rue de Paris. This traditional French bakery is located in a splendid Flemish renaissance house facing the Bourse. The sign outside claims that Paul was established in 1889, but this branch opened in 1996.

Practical information

Opening hours

The Palais des Beaux-Arts is open Wednesday-Sunday 10-6 and Monday 2-6. It is closed on Tuesday. The Musée de l'Hospice Comtesse is open Wednesday to Sunday 10-12.30 and 2-6 and Monday 2-6. It is closed on Tuesday, most French public holidays and during the first week of September. The Salle de Conclave on Place Rihour is open 1 April to 31 October, Monday to Saturday 9.30-12, 2-6, Sunday and public holidays 3-5. The Musée de l'Histoire Naturelle is open Monday to Saturday 9-12 and 2-5 and Sunday 10-5.

Travelling to Lille

The simplest way to reach Lille from Britain is by

Eurostar. The journey takes about 1 hour 40 minutes from London. Information: www.eurostar.com.

A high-speed TGV train runs from Paris Gare du Nord to the old Lille Flandres station in one hour. Information: www.voyages-sncf.com. The journey from Brussels Gare du Midi to Lille Europe takes 40 minutes, either by Eurostar or by high-speed Thalys trains. Information: www.thalys.com.

The nearest international airport is Paris Charles de Gaulle, 50 minutes by high-speed train from Lille Europe station. Brussels Zaventem airport is about one hour from Lille by train.

Air France flies to Lille-Lesquin airport, 7 kilometres from the city. Further information: www.airfrance.com.

Tourist information

The Lille tourist office is in the Palais Rihour, Place Rihour. Tel. 00.33.359.57.94.00 or internet www.lille-tourism.com. The French tourist office in London is at 178 Piccadilly, tel: 09068 244 123; and in New York at 444 Madison Avenue, tel 410 286 8310.

Tourist information is also available at www.franceguide.com.

Books on Lille

Just a few days before completing this book, I was sent a copy of Laurence Philips' *Lille* (Bradt mini guide, 2003). It just about made me weep. Philips has written a warm and witty guide to a city that he obviously loves. He is absolutely the person to guide you round the restaurants, bars and night clubs.

For those who can handle the French slang, the Petit Futé guide to Lille Métropole is stuffed full of addresses, though much of the information is for residents. The Guide Routard guide to Nord Pas-de-Calais has an excellent entry on Lille, which the authors concede is 'a city that is really changing, almost more so than Paris.'

Index

Cover illustration: L'estaminet-dînette by
François Azambourg, courtesy of Lille 2004
Title page, p. 22 and p. 84: details from map of Lille by Isaac Basire,
c. 1750, from History of England,
by Paul de Rapin-Thoyras
Photograph p. 11 courtesy of Conseil Municipal de Lille
Photograph p. 54-55 courtesy of L'Huitrière
Photograph p. 70 courtesy of La Bottega
Photographs p. 104, 110, 115, 118 courtesy of Palais des Beaux Arts
Photographs p. 144 (Les Arts Sauts), 163, 170 (Sunset over Paradise,
by L. C. Armstrong) courtesy of Lille 2004
Photographs p. 46-47 and 160 collection of the publisher
Other photographs collection of the author

First published 2004 by
Pallas Athene
42 Spencer Rise,
London NW5 1AP

WWW.PALLASATHENE.CO.UK

© Derek Blyth 2004
The moral right of the author has been asserted

ISBN I 873429 92 4

Printed in China